DOLLS HOUSES for Everyone

This is a fully illustrated beginner's guide to making, decorating and furnishing a single miniature room or a complete dolls house. Pat Cutforth assumes her readers have no carpentry, craft or design skills and her approach is based on simple techniques, shortcuts, and the anticipation of problems likely to arise.

The book suggests making a start on single room settings which don't require much furniture and can be attractively finished off with a picture-frame surround. A variant on these are Christmas scenes – framed, in a wreath or for the mantlepiece – and rooms for small animals like mice or badgers. Next Pat Cutforth tackles simple large-scale robust houses suitable for small children to use with their Sindy Dolls (or Action Men). She discusses the advantages and pitfalls of some of the dolls-house kits on the market, and then recounts what she learnt from building her own dolls houses. She is full of encouragement and practical hints if you want to design your own house. There are separate chapters on tools and techniques, lighting the houses by electricity, interior decorating, and making your own furniture. Full listings of dolls-house shops and suppliers are included and there are photographs, drawings and diagrams throughout, some of which can serve as actual templates from which pieces of furniture can be cut out.

This is a practical, realistic book which can be the entry to a magic world for your children and yourselves.

Pat Cutforth, an American by birth, lives with her husband and children on a farm in Wiltshire. Her first book, *Stripping Pine*, was published in 1983. She has taught a number of courses on dolls house making.

By the same author
STRIPPING PINE and other woods

DOLLS HOUSES
for Everyone

PAT CUTFORTH

John Murray

Photographs: Elizabeth Scott

© Pat Cutforth 1987
First published 1987
by John Murray (Publishers) Ltd
50 Albemarle Street, London W1X 4BD

Typeset by
The Castlefield Press, Wellingborough, Northants.
Made and printed in Great Britain
by Richard Clay Ltd, Bungay, Suffolk

British Library Cataloguing in Publication Data

Cutforth, Pat
    Dolls houses for everyone.
    1. Doll-houses
    I. Title
    745.592'3   TT175.3

ISBN 0-7195-4376-2

This book is dedicated to my family
for tolerating my obsessive dolls house phases
with such good humour

Acknowledgements

I would like to thank Liz Scott for taking so much trouble to get the photographs just right, Mary Flecker and Martha Holland for reading the chapters and giving me advice and encouragement, Lionel and Ann Barnard of The Mulberry Bush for their constant support, and finally my parents, who gave me my first dolls house, and have even turned into miniaturists themselves.

Contents

Introduction

Scratch a miniatures enthusiast and you may well find a deprived child: someone who envied their friends' train layouts or family dolls houses, while making do themselves with a circle of track on the floor, or a set of cardboard boxes. I was one of those deprived children, although my parents would be horrified to hear me say so. After all, they *did* give me a dolls house. It was a model of a 1930s semi-detached house – four rooms and an opening metal front pierced with window holes. The problems were that there were no stairs, or doors, or windows in the body of the house, and with only four rooms there was little space for furniture. Such furniture as I did have was plastic, so it was difficult to get bedclothes to stay on the beds, or people to stay on the chairs.

As I got older, I began to collect wooden furniture. I bought lots of bits and pieces even though the dolls house itself had passed on, and I had nowhere to keep it. For years I used to say that "my husband" would make me a dolls house, but when I found and married him I quickly realised that he was not the man for the job. So I bought myself a large old cupboard and a few tools, and set about making a dolls house myself. It took me a couple of years working on and off, but eventually it was finished, and I still love it, though I have become aware of its shortcomings. While I was working on it, my eldest daughter, Marguerite, showed a polite interest which I fostered in the belief that I was making it for her. Once finished, I found that her interest had evaporated – hardly surprising since I had given her no say in the decoration and furnishing. A year or so later I made her a Sindy house which was far more successful.

It's my belief that a great many mothers and fathers persuade themselves that they want to build a dolls house for their daughters, when they really want it for themselves. To find out if you are one of these parents, ask yourself the questions: "Has she shown any interest in dolls houses or asked to have one? Does she play with dolls?" If the answer to both questions is "No", then make one for yourself, and keep it in your hall or sitting room. It will look very decorative and attract hordes of adults who will give it all the admiration you could wish for. If your child has actually expressed a wish for a dolls house, then you might consider whether she wants a "good" one, which can grow with her, or whether she would be better off for the moment with a simple version designed around a favourite doll such as Sindy, Amanda Jane, or one of the countless other small dolls on the market. I will give some suggestions for this type of house in chapter 4.

One other idea for the beginning collector who has more enthusiasm than furniture, is to concentrate on a single room setting. This gives a focus to collecting, and there are many containers that can be adapted to the purpose.

You don't have to be a carpenter to make a dolls house or room box. When I started I didn't even know how to hold a saw. You can begin with a simple shape and upgrade later, or even buy a dolls house kit and learn the basics while putting that together. In the course of this book I shall assume that anyone reading it is about where I was when I started – keen but ignorant. The first few chapters will give ideas for a variety of one-room settings to get you started, then I will take you through the wood-working techniques that you need to make a dolls house from scratch or adapt a kit. Rather than give specific plans for one simple house, I have described my thoughts and conclusions in designing the dolls houses I have made, ranging from a large modern edifice for Sindy dolls, to a semi-detached terrace house with shop. Finally there are instructions for decorating and furnishing your finished house, with a list of dolls house shops and suppliers from which to supplement your own creative efforts.

1 · Miniature Rooms

If you have read my introduction and decided that you, and not your child, are the real dolls house enthusiast, then a good way to start is to make yourself a room box. These boxes are single framed rooms, usually between six and twelve inches deep (15 and 30 cm), which can be hung on the wall or slotted into a bookcase. They are marvellous for housing a small collection of miniature furniture, and can be decorated just like a room in a dolls house, thus giving you lots of practice for when you move on to something bigger. Even then, you will probably find that you still keep your original room to display favourite pieces of furniture, or to create a seasonal room setting – at Christmas, for instance.

Ready-made containers

One easy way to make a room box is to use a container that you already have. In the United States old clock cases have become so popular for this purpose that you can now even buy them in kits. Other possibilities are: a medicine cabinet, a small drawer, a basket, a small glass aquarium, a wooden box – or even a cardboard box. I have made some successful two-room settings as well, using double boxes, cupboards, sets of shelves, and the combination shelf and cupboard shown on the back cover.

When I first started on this hobby, my one idea was to avoid carpentry, because I had inadequate tools and little skill. I used any container I could find (even an old meat safe) and for my first room setting, I bought in an auction a glass-sided box of no obvious use, although a lingering smell made me suspect that it had housed mice, whether intentionally or not.

Framed boxes

Eventually I ran out of containers and took first to buying an old picture frame, then building a simple plywood box to fit behind. A local antique shop has a big stock of old frames and I root through these, looking for one that will suggest a certain atmosphere to me. A heavy old oak one might do for a shop, kitchen or attic, fine mahogany or pine for a bedroom, a more ornate gold one for a drawing room. One of the nicest I ever had was cut to size from an old birds-eye maple frame – but it was expensive.

When it comes to size, you should do some homework before you set off to buy a frame. Get your pieces of furniture, however few they are, and make a mock-up of your room around them. Use books, cardboard, anything to get a general effect of size and shape. Consider the eventual use of the room too: for example, a bedroom needs less height than a living room, and if you are making an old-fashioned kitchen, then you will find that a high ceiling gives the effect of a basement kitchen and also leaves room for hanging food like hams, and strings of onions. In buying frames for myself, I have found that 12″ by 10″ (30 x 25 cm) is a good all-purpose size, but those dimensions can be varied by several inches either way.

A room box ready for furnishing

If the prospect of hunting for old frames in junk shops and markets doesn't appeal to you, a simpler proposition is to make your box first and then take it to be framed. I don't do this myself because it is a lot more expensive, and also because I find that old frames inspire me – they seem to create a ready-made atmosphere, so that I can sense how I should decorate the room.

Making the Box

Now it's time to describe the making of the box. I use ¼" or ⅜" plywood, whichever will fit neatly into the rebate at the back of the frame (the rebate is the recess where the glass fits). You can instead use sturdy card, such as the Daler board sold in art supply shops for mounting pictures, and this you can cut with a Stanley or craft knife (I use one with snap-off blades for convenience).

If you decide to use plywood, then you will need some tools. Read chapter 5, p.52 on power jigsaws, and measure up for the plywood. Before you start, you need to decide on the depth of your room. I started by making them only four inches (10 cm) deep, which gave the effect of a three-dimensional picture on the wall, but I found that I was very limited as to the furniture that would fit. Since then my boxes have got deeper and deeper, finally settling at eight or ten inches (21 to 25 cm).

Besides your frame, you will also need:

- ¼" (6 mm) plywood. A piece 4' by 1' (120 x 30 cm) will do a 12" by 10" box eight inches deep
- glue, (I use a white wood-working glue like Evo-stick Resin W, or a glue-gun, but impact glue is probably easier for a first try)
- ½" panel pins
- hammer
- saw (power jigsaw or panel saw)
- fine sandpaper
- (optional: 1" hinges and glass plate for hanging)

First remove the glass, if there is any, from the frame, and measure the rebate – the two long sides first. Next measure the two short sides, subtracting twice the thickness of the wood, so that they will fit between the two long sides. Cut out these four pieces, as shown in the diagram on p. 14 and put them into the frame to make sure that they fit. Smooth all the wood with sandpaper, apply glue to the appropriate edges, and when it is tacky, put the box together. Strengthen these joints by nailing in panel pins.

You now have four sides, but no back. Put your open box into the frame and, keeping the frame on top, lay the box on the remaining piece of plywood to mark the back. Do this by drawing around the inside of the box with a very sharp pencil, and then cut along the outside edges of the pencil lines. This ensures a nice snug fit, and

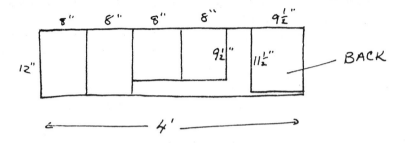

the piece should just slip into the back of the box: try it, then glue it in. (If it is loose, you can fill the gaps with glue.) Your box is now complete, so give the inside a coat or two of emulsion paint, stain or paint the outside of the box to match the frame, and then decorate it as if it were a room in a house (chapter 10).

If the frame fits snugly onto the box, then you can glue the glass back in and leave the frame unattached so it can be lifted on and off for rearrangment. You can also hinge the frame to one side of the box, the only problem here being a world scarcity of screws which are fat enough to hold a 1" (2.5 cm) brass hinge, but short enough not to protrude through the wall into the room. Ideally you need a ¼" (6 mm), size four screw, but failing that you will have to buy the more common ½" length and cut a bit off the end with a junior hacksaw – a very inexpensive tool (hold the screw by the pointed end in a pair of pliers or a vice while you saw).

If your frame has no glass, you have several options. You can glue the frame onto the box and leave it open, you can have a piece of glass cut to fit, or you can have a piece of sheet acrylic (used for double glazing) cut to fit. The acrylic is the best option if the box is to be given to a child.

A last step in construction is to fit a glass plate to the back of the box so that it can be hung on a wall. You will run into the same problem of the screws protruding through the wood, but this can be circumvented by having a chimney breast on the back wall (see chapter 10). If the box is to stand on a table or shelf, you will need to support it on a piece of scrap wood or a paperback, otherwise the frame will make it tip backwards.

Once you have the idea of this simple room box, you can begin to think about embellishments. Consider putting in a false wall, for instance. This can be made of plywood, of card, or of polyboard (foam core board) which is a quarter-inch thick sandwich of foam between two pieces of card.

Make your room slightly deeper (1 or 2 inches more), and install a false wall with a window cut in it (photo on p.21). Decorate this window with curtains, glaze it with thin sheet acetate, and put a scene on the back wall of the box so that it looks like a view seen through the window. Artists will have no problem painting such a scene, but apart from an attempt at primitive clouds, I have had to fall back for mine on postcards, or pictures cut from the Athena art catalogue. Mind you, it can be slightly disconcerting to look into a miniature room and see familiar Van Gogh cornfields outside the window.

There are lots of other things you can do with your false wall to create an illusion of life outside the room. I made an Edwardian-style kitchen once, and installed my false wall in one corner with a partly open door leading to a scullery. All that was visible through the door was a sink and a bucket and mop, but it added a whole other dimension to the room. I used the same technique in a maid's attic bedroom, but this time the door led out into a corridor where a dim light shone. The advantage of using a corner partition like this, is that it makes an attractive alcove on the other side and stops the room looking square and monotonous.

I have just mentioned using lights behind my false partitions, and I do feel that lighting adds immeasurably to the appeal of a room setting. It can be installed in the same way as lighting in a dolls house (chapter 6), with a small connector strip screwed onto the top or bottom of the box. Where you have false walls there must be some access to the light in case the bulb fails, so I usually cut a hole big enough for my hand out of the back of the box, and then tape card over it (make sure the hole is not visible from the front).

One slight snag that you may meet in wiring up a box with a 3.5/4 volts system is that the electrical current in the transformer may be too strong to run just one or two lights, because it is designed to support ten or twelve. If this is the case, the lights will shine very brightly and burn out after a day or so. To counteract this, buy some *resistors* from an electronics shop, such as Tandy. They cost only a few pence for a pack of five. Ask for 10 OHM resistors, 1/4 watt. Splice a resistor into one of each pair of wires on the back of your box, as shown in the drawing.

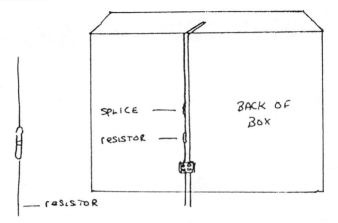

Having made your first box, you will probably find that you can't stop. They make marvellous presents for almost any occasion: imagine a little nursery scene to be used as a night-light for a new-born baby, a room full of personal belongings for a young person leaving school, or a kitchen as a present for a friend moving house. One that I made recently was for a Golden Wedding. I bought a small, 8" by 6" (20 x 15 cm), gold frame, and made a fairly shallow box, keeping the scale to the smaller 1/16 size (see p.96). Inside I had a corner fireplace with armchairs either side, and two old people sitting comfortably together. Over the fireplace was a Constable print of Salisbury Cathedral, to remind them of their home of many years, and all around were books and objects that were relevant to their life. I even made some clumsy golf clubs out of brown lumps of fimo stuck on sticks and mostly hidden by the golf bag, and was chagrined to see the most perfect set of golf clubs at a miniatures fair the other day. (For more on Fimo, see p.145.)

One very successful room was a large one set up as a badger's den. Because animals usually live in a single hole or nest, their dwellings lend themselves well to individual room boxes. I used papier maché (p.39), built up over a very rough frame of wood, to create twisting roots and little hollows. You can also make store cupboards up near the roof, alcoves for beds or tables, and tiny corridors ending in mysterious doors. Rabbits and mice have also provided ideas for miniature rooms, and I will go into this whole subject further in chapter 3.

Two nurseries made as presents

I have tried my hand at quite a variety of single rooms, many as presents, some on commission, and the main snag I have encountered is the expense of the furniture. For a while I bought the cheapest I could find, and painted or revarnished it, but eventually I took to mocking-up quite a lot of it. Going on the theory that the room would be treated more as a picture than as a dolls-house room, I made some of the larger features, such as wardrobes, so that they looked real but were fake. Drawer fronts were glued onto blocks to make chests of drawers, with large wooden beads for feet, beds were made out of cardboard boxes with draperies and bedding concealing the construction. This left money for the extras that are harder to fabricate, such as dolls, intricate furniture and china. There are more ideas in chapter 12, and you will find that your ability to invent and improvise will improve as you go along.

Vignettes

There is another development of this room box idea where mocked-up furniture comes in particularly useful, and this is in the very small scene known sometimes as a "vignette". A shallow box, such as a cigar box, is used to display a small grouping of items, generally without any figures. An example might be a potting bench strewn with tools, earth and pots, with a group of plants underneath. The bits and pieces are mostly glued in, since there is not really room for much rearranging of things once they are installed. Sometimes, instead of a box a glass dome is used, like the ones used to display stuffed birds. My father once won a prize at a miniatures show with one of these little scenes, but instead of the dome he used a Mexican glass box. He had entered a beautiful serpentine-fronted chest of drawers as an individual piece of furniture, but found he couldn't finish it in time. He did have another that he had made earlier to the same design, but the new one was to have tiny dovetails on the drawers and other refinements. In the end he set up both chests of drawers under the dome, the unfinished one lying about in pieces amidst wood shavings, and a roll of "plans" resting on the original one, so that it looked as if the carpenter had just stepped out in the middle of his work: true, in a sense, since the second chest never did get finished.

Miniature scene in a Mexican box

The Foldaway Box

There is one other simple idea for a single miniature room, which might be a solution for the timid. This is a box called a "foldaway box", made out of lightweight polyboard. When closed, it looks like a present, with a bow on top. Once the lid is removed, two of the sides fall down exposing the interior which is decorated like a small room. All the furniture has to be glued in place carefully, so that the pieces do not touch each other when the box is folded up. The various sections of the box, with instructions for making it, come in a kit which costs about £5, from Mini Mansions. As well as the basic one, there is also an outdoor scene with patio, and a shoe box size which provides a longer room. The instructions suggest vinyl paper as an overall covering for strength, but I think that fabric would be even better.

I will end this chapter with a list of rooms I have made to set you thinking up ideas of your own. In each case I found that it was the thought of the recipient and his interests or life-style that sparked off the idea for the subject of the room box.

Coffee Shop

This room was a present for some friends who had recently started up a coffee shop themselves, and I wanted to make it as like as possible. To narrow the scope, I concentrated on one section of the room, around the fireplace, which was of a Georgian design and which I reproduced fairly accurately with mouldings. Over the mantelpiece was a reproduction of a Breugel painting, and by a stroke of luck they had the very same painting in the Athena catalogue, so I was off to a good start. The walls of the shop I painted green, just like the full-size one. I had a black and white tiled floor, and curtains made of a tiny red and white print which approximated to the Habitat design on the real windows. For the inhabitants of the shop, I decided arbitrarily on a family of mixed animals, and they sat at little tables that I made out of wood to look as much like the real ones as possible: not difficult, because they were garden tables with a simple trestle structure. The china was made by spraying a plastic set with white car primer, then overpainting.

New York Apartment

This started out simply as a girl's room, as a present for my god-daughter on her confirmation. The New York part of it came when I was looking for a scene to put outside the window and found a New York skyline. From then on the room took off in my imagination, and I could picture how the girl lived in her one-room apartment, surrounded by books and plants. Apart from the bureau bookcase, I made all the furniture and furnishings myself, and the plans are given in chapter 12. The patchwork cushion on the armchair is a printed piece of Liberty lawn, and on the mantelpiece are some wooden animal ornaments which came from a bead shop.

For plants, I bought pots from an Oxfam shop, and ready-wired green fabric leaves from Toomers, a garden/seed/pet shop. I snipped the sides of these leaves so that they resembled a palm (the technique could equally be used to make a Swiss cheese or rubber plant) and then stuck them in some modelling clay, bending the leaves into graceful shapes. Beside the window wall is an alcove, and in this I glued shelves, filled with books made of strips of wood covered with Jollycraft gummed paper, and then cut into lengths (described more fully on p.141). I spent happy hours poring over magazines to find titles and tooling for the spines – occasionally hitting a bonanza, like a book club advertisement.

The room is lit with three lights, A Tiffany-style pendant over the desk, a red bulb in the fireplace, and a concealed light behind the false wall, illuminating the New York scene. This is one of my most successful rooms, and the only one I found it really hard to part with.

Converted shelves

My other goddaughter had inherited a set of furniture and dolls which had long been stored unused in a box. Her mother had the idea that I might be able to convert an old set of shelves to house this collection, and it turned out that the size was nearly perfect, since the furniture was in a very small scale, hardly 1/16th. The bottom of the two shelves had originally been a cupboard, but had lost its door, so I made a simple frame to fit the space, and decided that this bottom floor with its high ceilings should be a formal drawing room, with the top floor as a bedroom. I used fabric for wallpaper and soft, off-white paint to avoid any harshness that might clash with the old furniture, and added accessories of my own – paintings, ornaments, rugs. You can see these shelves on the back cover of this book.

Shop

This was commissioned as a teaching aid in schools, and was to be an old-fashioned village shop with post office. I decided on a fairly small room so as not to be swamped with making merchandise, and I set up two counters at right angles to each other, one being the post office. Behind the other counter stood the shopkeeper, a kindly grey-haired old man, and behind him were shelves of things for sale. There was also a set of drawers (false fronts) labelled "nibs", "writing paper" etc., all written with the finest pen I could find, after a bit of practice copying out some copperplate from an old farm ledger of ours. There was a door at the back of the shop leading to the owner's private premises, and a big shop window on one side wall, with a display counter behind it which was visible from outside.

Old-fashioned corner shop and post office

In the railway section of my local model shop, I found a series of packets called "Tiny Signs". Some of these are intended as travel signs for railway hoardings, and they were just the right size for postcards, stuck in a rack at the front of the post office counter. Other signs were advertisements, some containing pictures of packets of cigarettes and tobacco, which I cut out and stuck on boxes and round tins (all made from blocks of wood or short lengths of dowel). I made bars of chocolate – big ones like they used to be in the old days – by first covering a piece of wood with silver or gold paper, then wrapping it in coloured paper from the real bars of chocolate (purple from Cadbury's milk chocolate, red from

Bourneville). The trim and lettering was done with extra-fine gold markers, though the ink did tend to flow rather too freely.

The shelves at the back of the shop also held large bottles of sweets for sale. I bought some of the jars full of beads that toy shops sell, and filled them with liquorice sticks, humbugs, and other sweets made from Fimo. (Some surgeries and hospitals will let you have their empty inoculation bottles.) To fill up the remaining expanses of shelf, I made some large boxes, onto which I glued more of my labels, so they looked like the shopkeeper's extra stock. More signs, some from a sheet of railway hoardings for a larger scale of train, others cut from wrapping paper, were pasted round the room as advertisements. I also found some cinema posters: one advertising "The Silent Partner" at the Astoria I stuck on the side window. If you want to make an exterior sign to give the name of a shop, then I recommend Letraset rub-down transfer lettering, which is available in various fancy scripts and also in gold capital letters that look marvellous on a shiny dark green or red background.

Conservatory

I have included this because I am dying to make one. In the Hobby's catalogue I have seen a kit for a terrarium, made of glass and lead strips, which looks just like a conservatory. I can visualise it filled with plants, with a tiled floor, and a wicker table and chairs set out ready for tea. The plants could be fake, or better still real ones of an appropriate scale. There is a marvellous book called *Landscapes in Miniature*, by John Constable, which gives ideas for live plants that look right in a miniature setting.

Christmas

I find this theme so compelling that I have devoted a whole chapter to it, so read on.

2 · Ideas for Christmas

Christmas is a good time to start on miniatures. It conjures up the picture of an old-fashioned nursery with a dolls house in one corner, a Christmas tree surrounded by piles of presents, and stockings hung by the chimney: the whole atmosphere of anticipation and excitement can be created with a miniature Christmas scene, inside or outside a dolls house.

Christmas scene on a mantelpiece

My first attempt at one was a simple grouping of furniture and dolls on a mantelpiece. Little by little I added to this collection, progressing from a plain tree to a realistic one with lights, and picking up toys and accessories all through the year. Often I would improve some part of the scene as I put it away for the next year, because the rush before Christmas hardly leaves time for making real mince pies, let alone pretend ones out of Fimo. This year I had a 10" tall chimney breast at the back of my mantelpiece scene, and over it I made a sort of arched form out of chicken wire, which was the support for holly and ivy. Inside this wreath-like frame I placed some people and furniture stolen from my dolls house: a sideboard laden with food – Christmas cake, mince pies etc. – an armchair and rug to go by the fire, and a tree with presents and toys spread out underneath. On the rug sat my favourite dolls house girl holding a teddy bear: the teddy was replaced on Christmas day when I received a miniature Cabbage Patch doll made out of Fimo.

The fun of concentrating on one particular setting like this is that you can keep it in mind all year, and gradually build up a collection of bits and pieces without a huge initial outlay. After a while you might like to set it all up in a wreath. If you ask at your local delicatessen, they will probably give you one of the big round boxes that the larger cheeses like Dolcelatte come in: they are about 13" (33 cm) in diameter and 4" (10 cm) deep. Glue a shelf of heavy card or hardboard into this, about 3" (8 cm) from the bottom, to make a floor. Treat the inside of the wreath like a room in a dolls house, papering the walls, installing a chimney breast or other feature, and wrap the outside with chicken wire to support the greenery of your choice: ivy, spruce, whatever you prefer. When Christmas is over, you may find it hard to part with your wreath, but you can make it a permanent feature by using artificial ivy or preserved beech leaves for the outside, and changing the setting to suit the season.

My friend Sally and I made a Christmas wreath for her, two years ago, set up as a scene for mice. We made the wreath by bending hardboard around a circle of plywood and taping it, because I hadn't then discovered the cheese boxes, but curiously it ended up almost exactly the same size and depth. The walls we "papered" with sacking to give a rustic look, and we made a second floor overhead for a bedroom – rather cramped. I cut out a big farmhouse fireplace to Sally's design, and then she painted it and the floor most beautifully to look like stone. In fact she got so wound up in the whole project that she lay awake one night thinking the stones weren't quite right, and finally went down in her dressing gown to repaint them. There is a picture of this wreath and more about its decoration in chapter 3.

This year I was given a minute set of crèche figures from Mexico, the largest only ½" high. I was rather at a loss as to how to display them, and then hit upon the idea of using a round wooden box that had held turkish delight. It was 6" in diameter, and just over 1" deep, and I set it up liker the cheese box wreath, with a little floor made of hardboard. The "sky" I painted dark blue, with stars cut out of gold paper, and the largest of these had a grain-of-wheat bulb illuminating it, connected to a transformer plug (see chapter 6). I tied ivy around it and set the little scene inside. The whole thing only took a couple of hours to complete, and was most effective.

Here are some ideas and directions for dolls house Christmas decorations:

Tree

For a simple tree, buy one of the bristly ones that are usually around in the shops before Christmas, or look in your model railway shop for one of a suitable size. This year, after a lot of searching (all the trees seemed to be about ten inches tall, only suitable for a baronial hall), I found two packed together as Christmas tree decorations in British Homes Stores. To make your tree look like a real one, go to your nearest florist shop and ask for some green-dyed *erica moss* (lycopodium in the USA). Take your bristly tree, and starting at the bottom, insert pieces of the moss into the spikes of the tree, first dipping them in a spot of glue. As you work your way up the tree, make the bits of moss shorter, and leave the top ¼" bare. This technique makes a miraculously realistic tree, but it is quite a delicate structure, and I find that mine looks rather squashed and bedraggled after a year's storage. This time I stuck a few toothpicks into it before placing it in a box, hoping that they would hold it safely away from the sides.

For decorations I use beads, shiny red ones or opalescent ones in white, silver or gold. Sequins look very good, just stuck on with a dab of contact glue, and as well as round ones you can find sequins shaped like birds and stars. At a costume jewellery counter I once found a string of tiny gold beads, and this is wound round my tree, held in place at strategic points with glue. For the top of the tree, make an angel out of gold paper or foil (Melitta coffee bags are gold and silver reversible) from the pattern in the diagram. Make the skirt into a cone and glue shut. Or you could make a three-

Christmas tree made from erica moss

dimensional star from folded gold paper (origami experts only), or else glue on one of the sequins shaped like stars. Recently I found a little fairy at a miniatures show, and I now have her at the top of my tree. Looking at her closely, I find that her dress is a blossom from a spray of artificial flowers, turned upside down and dusted with iridescent glitter. The rest of her body is made from fine wire wrapped round with thread, she has a wooden bead for a head, paper wings, real silk hair, and a star sequin wand.

Other home-made decorations on my tree include candy canes made out of red and white Fimo wound together, and white snowflakes made out of quilling paper (quilling is a revived craft where thin strips of paper are wound tightly round a needle, and the resulting curls glued together to make patterns).

Pattern for a
Christmas tree
angel

TREE LIGHTS

Firstly I have to assume that your dolls house runs on a 12-volt system. Now, lights can be wired up in one of two ways: either in series or in parallel. The lights in the left-hand diagram are wired in parallel, and each bulb has a 12-volt charge. This is the system used for normal dolls-house lights. In the right-hand diagram, the lights are wired in series, and you add the voltage of the bulbs together to find the total – i.e. three 4-volt bulbs can be wired together in this way and plugged into a 12-volt system. Four of these bulbs add up to 16 volts, which gives a slightly dimmed light, quite suitable for a tree. Of course four Christmas tree lights would look a bit mingy,

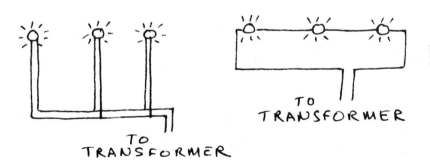

but you can make two strings to go round the tree and connect them into the plug together at the back. Buy the 4-volt grain-of-wheat bulbs (Lundby or Caroline's Home) sold in packs of two, and splice the wires together as in the diagram on p.66. Paint the wires green. The bulbs can be left clear, or painted in different colours with glass paints, or with the transparent acrylic paints available from model railway shops.

Paper chains

Sally and I tried and tried to make real paper chains for a Christmas scene that she made last year in an open three-sided box. I had the idea that we could roll up tubes of coloured gummed paper, cut them into rings, and then join them with more rings. We found the whole thing impossibly fiddly. In the end we used tinselly gold and red elastic ribbon sold for wrapping present, which we twined together and draped around the scene.

A Christmas scene in an open box

Since then, I have learnt how to make real paper chains using a quilling technique, and you can see some in the photograph of my mantelpiece scene (p.25). I cut narrow strips from the side of some brightly coloured writing paper – red, green, blue, yellow and white. Each strip was then wound round a toothpick to make it into a tight spiral. To make the loops, I used a piece of ¼" (5 mm) dowel as a form, and wrapped the first strip once round it, gluing the overlap. This loop was slipped off the dowel, and the next coloured strip inserted through it and wound round the dowel as before.

This loop by loop process is not as time-consuming as it sounds because the paper is already tightly curled, and I made the whole of the paper chain in the photograph in a couple of hours, watching television.

At a party before Christmas I discovered a great way of making streamers. I was given a "party popper" to let off, and stupidly held it the wrong way round so that the back exploded into my hand. When I looked at it, curled up inside was a collection of tiny rolls of different coloured paper. When I pulled the middle out of one of these, a perfect little spiral unrolled and, wound together, the spirals looked like garlands of streamers.

Presents

These are tremendous fun to make, and children can help. Cut some scraps of wood, dowelling, balsa or styrofoam into blocks of different shapes and sizes. Wrap these just as you would a full-size present, gluing the ends shut. Real wrapping paper can be found with suitably small designs, or use plain coloured foil or gummed paper.

ENLARGEMENT

For ribbon I recommend the cheap shiny stuff that can be torn into strips. First wrap a thin (about 1/16" – 2 mm) piece round the box, just as you usually would, and glue the ends down. Then take another strip and make a bow by weaving it back and forth onto a pin as in the drawing, giving it the occasional twist to make a loop stand up. Finally snip the end off the pin with your pliers and press the head and the bow into the piece of wood. If you want to make a real tied bow, either for a package or for the tree, then tie it round the teeth of an "afro" comb held upside down in a vice.

Wreaths

Perfect miniature pine cones grow on alder trees. These moisture-loving trees are usually found with willows, hanging over rivers and canals. For the base of a wreath, cut a circle of paper or green felt, and then stick the cones in place, filling in any gaps with suitably sized seed heads, pickling spices, clusters of red beads, Fimo applies or anything else you can think of use tweezers if your hands are all thumbs. Tie a bow on, if you like, made like the ones for presents, on p.31. Wreaths are quick and fun to create, and they make a good Christmas present for a friend with a dolls house.

Food

A Christmas pudding can be made out of Fimo. Dribble some white paint over it for icing, and make a sprig of holly from green paper and red beads or dots of red Fimo. To ice a Christmas cake, first put on a layer of Fimo marzipan, then use very thick white paint or Fine Surface Polyfilla (spackle) for the royal icing. The strips of embossed gold paper sold for edging wedding cakes usually have some bits that are small enough to be cut out and wrapped round the cake: tie a ribbon round the paper to finish. On the top you can have Fimo figures and Christmas trees made from the tops of the smallest model railway or cake decorating trees.

Yule log

This decoration for table or mantelpiece can be made from a small section of bark, or a twig. Into it you can stick a thick red candle made from a painted length of ¼″ dowel, or three thin ones in a row (cut these from toothpicks, the centre one slightly taller than the other two). Decorate these logs like the wreaths with beads, model railway greenery, and a red or green bow on the front.

Stockings

To hang by the chimney with care. My mother has knitted me some red and green ones on her smallest needles, each with a white top. You can also cut them out of felt, and paint or stick on decorations. If you prefer to have them filled, then stuff them with cotton wool and choose some tiny toys or candy canes to stick out of the top.

Toys

The best and cheapest source of toys for your miniature scene is the Christmas decoration department of a large department store. In this way I have found perfectly scaled sleds, airplanes, wagons, bicycles, teddies, rocking horses, toy trains, drums, trumpets and other musical instruments: it's like a treasure hunt. Some of the toys are crudely made and look better repainted, but often they have good detail, and they are usually very inexpensive – especially in the sales after Christmas! You can make lots of toys, like building blocks cut from lengths of balsa or obechi strips sold in model shops, a skipping rope with bead and toothpick handles, or a toy farm using HO-scale railway accessories. (More in chap. 12.)

Sometimes one special item helps set the scene, and this year great excitement was caused by a little box I bought at the Mulberry Bush in Brighton. The words "red shoes" were written on the end of the box, and inside, nestling in tissue paper, was the most adorable pair of red children's shoes, barely half an inch long.

Christmas cards

These can be cut from the many charity gift catalogues that arrive before Christmas. Place them on the mantelpiece, or glue them onto strips of ribbon to hang on the wall.

There is one other idea for a Christmas scene which I am longing to try. It would be a great project for a family that included model railway enthusiasts as well as dolls house lovers, because it is a miniature village, set out with a winter scene. I want to make it in N-scale, which is the smallest commonly available, so that the whole thing could stand on a shelf or be a table centrepiece. This project could be one that grows from year to year: just a few buildings to begin with, perhaps some village houses grouped round a pond – frozen, of course, with ice skaters starting out on it. I have heard that bicarbonate of soda (baking soda) makes good snow, if you have the courage to face the supermarket queue with what looks like a life supply of the stuff. You paint the base of your scene with glue, sprinkle on the baking soda, and then spray it with art fixative to prevent drifting. In it you can press the feet of your tiny villagers to make footprints, showing the paths they have taken as they walk home with their packages.

The next year more people could be added, a hill with children sledding, a church lit for an evening service, or perhaps a farm. There are endless possibilities.

I hope to leave you encouraged to try some small scene for

3 · Mouse Houses

Under this heading I include any animal dwelling, like the badger house shown on page 38. I know that many people find dressed-up animals quite revolting, but children love them: witness the success of books like Beatrix Potter's, the Little Grey Rabbit and Brambly Hedge series. The great thing about making a room for an animal, or animal family, is that all the different parts of their lives can be shown at once – sleeping quarters, living area, food stores, etc. It's cosy and cluttered, and wonderful for children to play with.

Two Mouse Houses

My first excursion into the animal world was with some mouse houses, built round a series of small mice that I found in a gift shop. They were less than two inches tall, so their accommodation fitted into a very small container, about the size of a cigar box. I put no lighting in these houses because they were too shallow for lights to show, and I kept the decoration simple. They were fun to make and could be completed in a couple of afternoons, making them

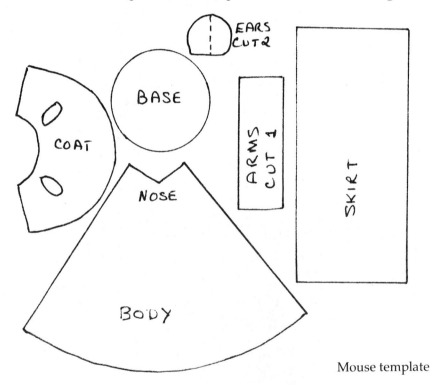

Mouse template

ideal presents for a godchild or a new baby. I have included a photograph of two of these houses, and you will see that they depend for their atmosphere on the choice of a suitable cosy fabric for the walls, and on mousey accessories, liks sacks and food. I have drawn a simple pattern for making a mouse out of grey felt, and you can embellish him with eyes made from black beads or painted on (use felt tips), and whiskers made of thread (droopy) or fishing line (bristly). To construct the mouse, cut out 1 base, 1 body, 1 arm, and 2 ears from grey felt. The clothing can be felt or fabric. Make the body into a cone by oversewing the two front edges together, then sew the nose shut. Stuff firmly and oversew the base to the bottom edges. To make the head, tie some strong thread tightly around the body, 1.5 cms from the nose. Pull the head forward slightly by running a line of gathering stitches along the front seam from nose to neck. To make the arms, stick the felt arm piece around a piece of pipe cleaner, then make a hole right through the mouse's body and push the arms through. Fold the ear pieces in half, and stick the lower edges together. Glue them to the mouse's head. There is a coat pattern too, to make from felt, or if you want a woman, wrap her up in a shawl, like the badger mother on p. 38. Sack and basket instructions are at the end of this chapter.

More ambitious than these little mouse houses was a Rabbit Room that I made for a goddaughter's christening. To add a bit of interest to the box-like room, I set the fireplace at an angle across

A Rabbit Room

the corner, and added a round window in one of the side walls. The mother rabbit is reading to her child, with a lot of baking and cooking preparation set out on the kitchen table. There was no room for beds, but I squeezed in quite a few sacks and baskets to store food, and tried to make the room interesting with details – pictures on the walls, false beams glued on here and there. I think now that it is a bit small to be satisfactory as a toy – it works better as a picture, or a night light.

By far my most exciting animal creation was the badger room I made for a little girl who collects badgers of all sorts. This room was much bugger than any I had attempted before, and took quite a time to finish, because I made so much of the furniture and accessories myself. I started with a box 15″ by 10″ (38 x 25 cm) and 9″ (23 cm) deep, and in it I wedged some roughly shaped pieces of plywood, as a framework for papier maché tree roots. (Instead of plywood you could use pieces of styrofoam packing; look outside your local electrical shop on the day the municipal rubbish

The Badger Room

collectors come round.) In placing the tree roots, I had a rough plan
of the separate areas that I wanted to create in the room: one with a
table and chairs, one around the fireplace, another with a bed and
a storage niche overhead. I glued the plywood in, and then covered
it in papier maché made in the following way:

Papier maché

You need:

- newspapers
- Evo-stick Resin W woodworking glue, or other white glue
- water
- paints (household emulsion as a base, then posters or water-
  colours for the final painting)
- brushes (for painting, and a 1" one for applying glue)
- varnish (any)

Tear the newspaper into rough pieces about 2" (5 cm) square. Pour
some glue into a bowl or saucer and dilute it with water (about half
and half). Paint one side of a piece of newspaper liberally with the
glue, and stick it onto your framework, then repeat with more
newspaper, tearing pieces into suitable sizes where necessary
(long strips to wrap round corners, etc.). This part goes very
quickly and you will soon become adept at slapping on glue and
sticking the pieces in place. When the framework is all covered and
you have built the shapes to look the way you envisaged, let the
whole thing dry completely. This will take some hours, because of
all the layers of wet glue and paper.

When the papier maché is dry, give it a couple of coats of
emulsion paint, so that the newsprint is covered up. Then paint on
two coats of poster paint of a suitable colour, or of two similar
colours (mid and dark brown for instance – when you rub the top
coat, as I will describe in a moment, the first coat will glimmer
through). When all the paint has dried, take a damp cloth or paper
towel and rub the top coat lightly, so that the texture of the papier
maché shows through, giving it a rough woody effect. Finally, give
the whole thing a coat of varnish to preserve it, using matt varnish
if you don't like a shiny surface.

With the papier maché walls completed, I installed a fireplace and two doors made of card, one with a couple of steps leading up to it. The furniture in the room, apart from the armchair, was made from wood, all to the most simple designs, as you can see from the photograph. I also had to make two badger children, which turned out to be rather fun, although I was dreading it. I had the mother already, and I studied her and then simplified the design, pushing pipecleaners, for arms, right through the cone-shaped bodies. The distinctive markings I made with black felt tip pens on the white felt bodies, and I dressed them in some simple wrap-around clothes. The lighting was in the alcoves, to add to the mystery of the room, and there was a red-painted bulb in the fireplace.

A Mouse House in a wreath

A very impressive Mouse House was made by Sally (with my help), originally as a Christmas scene in a wreath, as described in chapter 2. The idea came from a cover of Nutshell News magazine, which was based in its turn on a Brambly Hedge picture. We made two floors in the wreath, giving one large main room, a small arched overhead bedroom, and a storage area at the very bottom. We used wallpaper paste to stick rough sacking to the walls, and I cut a chimney breast out of an offcut of pine (other ways of making chimney breasts are on page 109). Sally painted stones around the opening of the hearth and on the hardboard floor, using water-colour paints in soft greys and beige.

After the construction came the fun. Sally already had a couple of mice and a few bits of furniture in 3/4 scale. One was a dresser which she didn't like because it was made of raw-looking wood, but painted off-white and loaded with food it looks marvellous. She made a trestle table, and a round covered table out of a jar lid resting on a spool, dipping the tablecloth in wallpaper paste so it could be moulded to a suitable shape. (Fuller directions on page 139.) Upstairs we had a four-poster bed made out of a cardboard box and four lengths of dowel (pencils would do), with curtains tied round them to conceal all but the shape. This was later removed because it was a bit too big. We cut mouse pictures from wrapping paper and cards, and framed them with small brass curtain rings and washers. A few beams were added to the ceiling of the main room, mainly as a support for hanging strings of onions and bunches of dried seed heads. Collecting the things which serve as provisions is one of the charms of these mouse scenes. You can raid the kitchen cupboards for rice, lentils, and pasta shapes, and go for long walks to hunt for acorns, berries and seed heads.

Baskets

You can buy little baskets at miniature shows and dolls house shops, and they are not expensive, but to supplement them, here is an easy method for making many different shapes of baskets.
You need the following:

- natural coloured needlepoint canvas, with 16 to 18 threads to the inch

- forms on which you can shape the baskets (blocks of wood, dowel, medicine bottles)
- elastic bands

Sacks, and baskets, and baby mouse in a walnut shell

Cut a piece of needlepoint canvas about 3″ square (8 cms), and wet it thoroughly. This releases the glue in the canvas which will eventually make it hold the basket shape when it dries again. Place the end of one of the forms – let's say a piece of dowel – in the centre of the canvas, and press the edges up the sides of the dowel, easing the canvas into place so that there are no lumpy overlaps. Put an elastic band around the top to hold it while it dries (see centre of photo). When it is quite dry, slip it off the dowel, and trim all the edges of the canvas level with scissors. Or cut it with a craft knife while it is still on the dowel.

To finish, pull a thread off the large piece of canvas and wet it. Wrap it round the top of the basket to give a neat edge. A handle can be made of several strands wound or plaited together. In all the basket construction you should find that the size in the canvas is all the glue you need – it stiffens beautifully when dry, and you can hold handles and trim in place with clothes pegs or paper clips while you wait. The form for the basket can be any size and shape you like, and you will find the construction simple and quick; children can handle it easily.

LOG BASKET

We made a log basket by cutting about 2" off a cardboard tube (from a roll of toilet paper), and wrapping this round with rough twine soaked in white glue. It looked messy to begin with, but dried clear. A length of string was made into two long loops that went up both sides of the basket handles. You can just see the basket to the right of the seated mouse in the photo on p. 40. We drew round the tube on a piece of card to make the bottom of the basket.

Sacks

Another essential accessory for Mouse Houses. A group of sacks is more fun if you use lots of different materials like hessian, unbleached calico, sheeting, openweave cotton in earthy colours, and so on. I rarely bother to sew them, instead I cut out a rectangle anywhere between 4" by 6" (10 x 15 cm) and 2" by 3" (5 x 8 cm), depending on the size I want. I make this into a tube, overlapping the two short sides and gluing them shut (use white glue). The bottom edge is also overlapped and glued, and the top I just fray slightly and roll down. You can also make a flour sack out of white cotton or unbleached calico, tying the corners with string, and writing on the front with felt tips.

Many gifts and craft shops carry felt animals which are in 1" to 1' scale, and you may enjoy working around this standard dolls house size. However, I find that a slightly smaller scale gives more scope for the one-room dwelling, and makes it easier to create that cosy, cluttered look that we have come to associate with mice especially. The Brambly Hedge books will give you lots of ideas for the rooms themselves, and for furniture, turn to chapter 12 and try reducing the patterns by a third on a photocopier, so that they will suit a person of 4" rather than 6". If you want to use 2" people or animals, reduce the patterns again.

You can be more flexible about the size and shape of mouse rooms than dolls house rooms. Let your eye be your judge, and extend the height of the room by several inches if you want one of those cavernous Brambly Hedge kitchens, or bring the ceiling right down for a more intimate den-like effect. If you decide on a low ceiling, it is a good idea to make the room a bit shallower so you can reach in.

In the smallest scale, where your animals are only 2″ high, you can afford to have several rooms – a sort of mini dolls house – and still take up very little space. Think of burrows, and dens, and runs. Start with one main room, like my badger house, and add little rooms around it, like a slice through the middle of a hillside. After all, no-one really knows what goes on underground, and imagining it, and realising your imaginings, is the fun of creating these mouse houses.

4 · Sindy Houses

My older daughter, Marguerite, was never interested in my dolls house, but she had a vast collection of Sindy and Barbie dolls and their accoutrements, so finally I decided to make her a Sindy house. This required some thought, because a 12" doll requires a pretty monstrous edifice in order to have all the necessary rooms. Just at the right moment, I found a design in a Sunset publication *Things to Make for Children*, which was called "Four Story Doll House". It was just what I was looking: a modern open-plan design with a lift on one side, well suited to the dolls' teen-age image, and using vertical space instead of spreading sideways. A list of wood and parts was given with the instructions, along with the statement that it could be built in two or three evenings. I would like to say that for me at least, this was not the case, and I was still fixing on the roof balcony at a quarter to two on Christmas morning.

The house was a great success, and gradually we furnished it. The bottom floor was a garage in the original design, but we raised the ceiling and turned it into a kitchen. Marguerite chose a patterned Fablon for the floor, and we bought some of the excellent plastic Sindy kitchen units. I made an Aga cooker out of a block of wood. It had one opening door, and lids that lifted up to reveal cooking rings. Along the front of the cooker I put the characteristic rail, made out of a length of dowel, painted with aluminium paint and supported by two screw-eyes. We had a very simple wooden table and chairs, and I also made a sort of side table to hold extra food and china.

As we continued to collect and make furniture, we discovered that quite a lot of metal and brass souvenirs come in just the right size for Sindy. We found an old-fashioned telephone which was really a pencil sharpener, a tiny oil lamp that actually worked (under supervision, of course), a brass wind-up gramophone, and lots of dolls house food, including a box of tins of soup.

The middle floor was a big bedroom. I made two wooden beds and varnished the chipwood floor so that it could have rugs.

The Sindy house

Storage of Sindy clothes is a major problem, so we had two wardrobes and a chest, which was really a small wooden box of mine. The tall top room was the sitting room, and was mostly furnished with some simple modern chairs. They consisted of two blocks of wood, glued at right angles, then slightly padded, and covered with corduroy to resemble those big foam loungers that were so popular a few years ago. A prized acquisition was the Sindy Music Centre which incorporated a real radio.

The one area that was a bit of a flop was the balcony, which was so high that Marguerite, age 8, could hardly reach it. The lift (elevator) had a short life too, but that was because I made it out of hardboard instead of plywood, so it came apart (hardboard is hopeless for gluing and screwing – I rarely use it). The lift worked on a clever principle. There were magnetic cupboard catches screwed to the outer wall in each floor, and the lift, which ran up and down in grooves in the side wall, had a matching magnet so that it could stop on each floor. I used a router to cut the channels in the side walls, but you could also use the "groove" edge of tongue and groove boarding, which is available in various thicknesses. (The lift has been renewed for the photograph. It is on the left, behind my daughter.)

Marguerite added touches of her own: floor cushions, curtains, a covered table. After a while we electrified the house with a simple system of overhead lights made from ping pong balls, and a couple of lamp sockets. (Incidentally, excellent, inexpensive Sindy electric lights and lamps, made by the German firm Hahn, are available from some toy shops, including Hamleys in London and Tridias in Bath.) Our Sindy house was admired by children and parents and copied several times, so that look-alikes are dotted around Wiltshire.

A similar building could be designed to suit Action Man (who is the same height) with features more suited to manly or military premises. Some basic furniture is available for Action Man, and a handy boy could mock up tables and stools. The project would be fun for frustrated mothers with no daughters, especially since boys are often just as interested in miniatures as girls, as shown by the constant popularity of model railways, forts and farms, and the little "Play People" with their castles and ships. My brother spent far more time designing the layout and scenery for his model railway than he did running the trains.

A friend of mine who lives in Ireland made a very good Sindy house out of wine crates discarded by a wine merchant. When I asked for some locally, I was told that nearly all the bottles now come in blister packs, and that my only hope was to find a wine buff who might be laying down vintage wine for investment.

If you can get hold of these boxes, you can arrange them in many different ways, and add to them as need dictates. You may want to cut windows and archways through from room to room, and divide the sections by a staircase, or keep it simple as in the plan of my friend's house, shown in the drawing, where the roof is an addition that creates an attic bedroom. There is a modern front to this house, cut from plywood and held with magnetic catches, but it is not strictly necessary.

If you are interested in the Sindy size, but too nervous to make a

house, then you might start with a one-room apartment. A large sturdy cardboard box would do, and doors and windows could be cut in it with a craft knife. Better still, make a simple box out of plywood, as described in chapter 1, but remember that it must be at least 14″ (35 cm) high to take these taller dolls. The depth of a Sindy room also needs to be greater than in a dolls house, or the furniture won't fit in, but more than 16″ (40 cm) becomes inaccessible. Make the room as wide as you like – my Sindy rooms were 29″ (74 cm) across. As a general rule for size, work on the principle of 2″ equals 1′, letting your eye be your guide. For example a 5′ (152 cm) kitchen table would be 5″ (13 cm) long in a normal dolls house, and should be 10″ (25 cm) long in a Sindy house. In practice this is rather large, and an 8″ (20 cm) table looks more appropriate. Don't forget that any fireplaces, windows, or other built-in components need to be twice as tall as in 1″ scale. It can be quite a problem keeping to the larger size if your eye is already "in" on the dolls house scale.

A few years ago we found we needed more space in my younger daughter Eleanor's room, and as she was showing no interest in Marguerite's Sindy house, we decided that it could be handed on to another family on a long-term loan. Needless to say, about a week later she wanted it back, and from then on we had a series of improvised Sindy houses. She used a cupboard, emptying all its contents out onto the floor every time it was needed for Sindy. I made a second, cottage-style house which was far too small, being only 13″ deep (I don't know what I was thinking of – dolls houses,

I expect). Then I devised what I thought was a brilliant and adaptable plan. I made five wooden panels out of ⅜" (1 cm) plywood, each one 15" high by 20" long (38 x 50 cm). In one I cut an arch, in another a window, in still another a door. Each panel had screw eyes in one end and cup hooks in the other. My ideas was that they could be hooked together in lots of different combinations, incorporating the actual walls of Eleanor's bedroom as well, and stacked neatly away when not in use. To begin with, all the panels were painted white, then we decided to paint and paper them to make them more interesting, and from then on they were useless because the versatility was lost. In retrospect I do think this would have been a successful system if I had left the panels white, and also added about two more. If you think about it, even standing them in the corner of a room, you can't make more than two complete Sindy rooms out of five panels.

The fun of these Sindy houses lies in their modern style. The planning of a London flat, or teenage "pad" inspires a kind of creativity that is very different from the designing of a traditional dolls house. You may find that some of the patterns given in chapter 12 are suitable in style, although they will have to be enlarged. Ask a photocopier to double them. Modern fitted furniture, with its simple lines, is easy to make out of wood or stout card. For instance, a "platform bed" could be a rectangle of plywood glued into a corner of the room, and supported underneath by blocks of wood. Cover it with a shaggy rug made from fur fabric (tiger skin perhaps?), and lots of cushions. Incidentally, when we make Sindy floor cushions we fill them with rice or pearl barley, so that they are heavy like a bean bag. If you are short on ideas, look at illustrations in magazines or furniture catalogues (Habitat, for instance) and don't worry about fine points: cupboards can be left open, without doors, tables made of a flat slab of wood with four legs glued to the corners.

There is lots of scope for using "found" objects in Sindy furnishing, like the plastic box that Ferrero Rocher chocolates come in, recycled as a perspex coffee table, or an empty photo display cube as an end table. All the pictures in Marguerite's Sindy house were either postcards of modern art, or illustrations cut from magazines and left unframed.

Take a good look at the plastic Sindy furniture, because although some, like the bedroom furniture, is pretty tacky, much of it is realistic and good value. The kitchen units are excellent, particularly the sink and the stove, and there is an irresistible set of patio equipment. Visitors to the Sindy house might be accommodated in the caravan, or you could use the sleeping bag from the camping kit.

These Sindy houses are an excellent interim dolls house substitute for children under nine or ten. The larger size of the rooms and furniture make it easy for their small hands to move things around, and even for them to make their own furniture. You, the adult who really wants a dolls house, will find you are able to keep your hands off a Sindy house, and won't have to choke down reproofs when the walls are redecorated with felt tips. Because I didn't really mind how Marguerite decorated the Sindy house, I was able to work with her and help her make things, without constantly saying, "Here, let me just do that bit for you". I think we both look back on it with fond memories.

5 · Tools and Techniques

This chapter is for reference and general information. I thought it would be distracting if I broke off in the middle of describing the construction of a building to discourse on power jigsaws and glues. I will list the tools and supplies that I use, plus some alternatives, and describe my basic construction techniques.

Talk to any of the craftsmen at a miniatures show, and they will probably tell you that they use full-size tools, the reason being that they are more powerful and accurate than the tools made especially for miniature work. Even less accurate, and often positively dangerous, are the tools sold for children. With the exception of the hammer, toy tool-kits have blunt, shoddy tools which are difficult to control, and inclined to slip suddenly because of the effort required in using them. What I am really saying is that my tools are full-size adult ones, with the exception of the miniature mitre box and saw. Most of them will be in your tool chest already, and none of them are expensive except the power jigsaw, which you can hire.

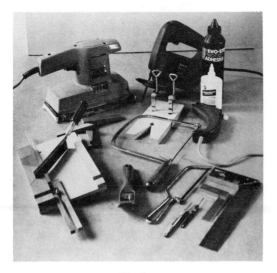

Tools

Saws

There is no doubt that plywood can be cut with an ordinary panel saw, but it is a long and tedious process. There seems to be an inverse logic about tools, so that the simpler they are, the more skill they require. I myself use a power jigsaw (hand-held sabre saw) for almost all my wood-cutting, and I have recently progressed from a bottom-of-the-range Black and Decker, to a more powerful jigsaw with a tilting soleplate so that I can make angled cuts. It is a Bosch, but many firms make a comparable one. To get acquainted with one of these power jigsaws, I recommend hiring one for a day (look in the Yellow Pages for hire firms). Hiring is a surprisingly reasonable process, and you will be able to use a good quality saw that you would find expensive to buy. Ask for blades suitable for plywood, and giving a "clean cut". This last is very important – with the right blade you will have a smooth finished edge, instead of the ragged splintery one usually associated with plywood.

Some people will consider that power tools are too dangerous to use, and I certainly would not let a child near one, but providing that you take due care and observe obvious safety rules, like keeping your fingers away from the blade, you should come to no harm. I have done much more damage to myself with a Stanley knife than ever I have with power tools.

When using your power jigsaw, there are one or two rules for easy handling. Firstly, always keep the soleplate (the metal base plate) firmly on the wood. If you lift it, the wood will vibrate with a terrifying noise. It follows from this that when you want to remove the saw from the wood to change direction, you must first turn it off. Actual cutting techniques are on the next page.

If you prefer not to use a power jigsaw, then I recommend that you take your measurements to a timber yard or well-equipped Do-It-Yourself shop, and get them to cut the main pieces to size. Make sure that they do their cutting on a proper saw with a fence for accuracy – you would be amazed at how many timber yards cut up their wood with a panel saw or a hand-held jigsaw following a rough line. Without a power jigsaw, any windows will have to be cut with a *keyhole saw* (a blade can be purchased to fit into a Stanley knife handle) after first drilling holes in all four corners of the area to be cut out.

CUTTING WITH A POWER SAW

If you order a full sheet of ⅜" (1 cm) thick plywood it will measure 8' by 4'. British timberyards are still a hopeless muddle of metric and imperial measures, so you can find yourself asking for, say, a two-metre length of 3" by 1". When your sheet arrives, don't try to cut it flapping about on your kitchen table; instead, lay it on the floor, do all your marking out (check and recheck), and then prop it up underneath with offcuts of wood. The object is to raise the section of plywood that you are about to cut, just enough so that the saw will clear the floor. You only need your props under either side of the line you are going to cut first. Try to cut the sheet more or less in half to begin with, to make it less unwieldy.

The advantage of having the sheet of plywood propped up on the floor is that you can crawl along it as you cut and aren't forced to saw at full stretch. It is only when I get to the last few cuts, when the pieces are a couple of feet long, that I remove them to my Workmate (a portable workbench which supplements my main workbench – the kitchen table). If you have no bench, I recommend doing all the cutting on the floor, even the windows.

I will repeat here my earlier injunction to get the right blades for your jigsaw. For the Bosch I get T 101B and for Black and Decker I recommend A 5041 or A 5046, or the Professional quality A2204. You will need at least one pack of five blades to cut out an entire dolls house, because the glue in plywood blunts the blades very quickly. A blunt blade means a rough cut.

To make a hole in the middle of a piece of wood, for a window, for instance, first drill a hole in one corner, big enough so that you

CUT ALONG
DARK LINES LAST

can insert the saw blade. When cutting into corners, the technique I use is shown on p. 53. I cut right into the first corner, then back up and swing round in a tight curve so I can cut into the next corner. When you have gone all the way round the window the central piece of wood will drop out, but you are left with small wedge-shaped bits in each corner. Turn the jigsaw around and cut these from the other direction.

FRETSAW

A great tool for the miniature furniture maker, the fretsaw has a very fine blade which lets you cut all sorts of complicated shapes. You can buy a complete kit with fretsaw, blades, boring tool, cutting table and clamps for just over £5 from Hobby's. To cut out a shape, you rest the work flat on the special cutting table which has a V-shaped hole cut in it to allow the saw to move up and down.

The boring tool included in the kit is used to drill a small hole when you are cutting an opening, like a window, in the middle of a piece of wood. Once the hole is drilled, remove one end of the blade from the fretsaw frame, and thread it through the hole in the wood before starting the cut.

Electric fretsaws are a luxury for the committed miniaturist but you can still get an old-fashioned treadle one from Hobby's. They enable you to cut out really complicated shapes easily, with both hands free to manoeuvre the wood. Here again, the larger, more powerful tools are really the best buy. I have a Swiss magnetal fretsaw which was not very expensive, but I find that it is too weak to be truly accurate: I end up with wavering cuts that need a lot of filing and sanding. I really prefer my full-size Burgess bandsaw, although it won't turn as sharply as a fretsaw. Newer versions of my bandsaw are now available with an optional fretsaw attachment.

JUNIOR HACKSAW

This small tool is available from Woolworths or any hardware store for about £1. It will do all your metal cutting, from brass tubing for curtain poles to decorative strips for grates and fenders. Handy for cutting full-size curtain rails too.

Knife

I recommend a craft knife with replaceable or snap-off blades. You will find you can even use it to make straight cuts in wood (not plywood) up to 3/16" thick, holding the knife firmly against a metal ruler, and scoring along the cut several times.

Carpenters Square

This tool is for marking lines that are exactly square to the edge of a board. Inexpensive squares can be bought from Woolworths, some of them with markings for cutting 45% angles for mitres.

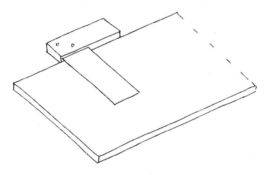

A machinist's square is a small metal version of the carpenter's square, and it would be extremely useful for miniature work were it not prohibitively expensive. Instead, for checking and marking angles, I use a set square or protractor like the ones sold in geometry sets, but I must emphasise that you need good ones with nice sharp corners. Buy them in an artists' or draughtman's supply shop.

Rulers

I use a steel rule for marking general measurements, and a transparent twelve-inch ruler for detail. This transparent ruler, on which the markings go right across the width, is particularly useful when making templates for windows and doors, because you can see when your lines are parallel.

Dividers

The dividers that come in every geometry set are extremely useful in miniature work, for transferring measurements. For example, when you are measuring for skirting boards in a dolls house, instead of groping inside with a measuring tape, take the dividers and spread them out so that the points reach into the two corners of the wall. Carefully remove the dividers without disturbing them, and then prick your strip of moulding to show you exactly the length you need.

You can use this same technique to ensure that the four legs of a piece of furniture are the same length, or the two sides of a picture frame. It is much more accurate than taking measurements with a ruler.

Miniature Mitre Box and Saw

This is an invaluable pair of tools. The box is made of metal and has slits in it which hold the saw in the right position for making angled cuts, for picture frames, for example. There is also a slit for a straight cut, and this is useful for cutting out pieces of wood for furniture. I strongly recommend buying a mitre box and the fine-toothed saw that comes with it. X-acto make one that is carried by most model shops, or you can get a very small one from Hobby's for under £2.

A refinement on the basic mitre box is the excellent cutting jig designed and sold by Lionel Barnard of The Mulberry Bush. You can see it on the left in the photo (p. 51), used with an X-acto saw. As well as the usual slots for straight and angled cuts, it also has adjustable stops to let you cut several pieces to the same length, and a collection of wedges to hold glued pieces together firmly while they dry.

Drill

I have a power drill, but there is no reason why you cannot use a hand one.

Pin Vice

This is a small tool like a stubby pencil with a chuck in one end that tightens to hold very small drill points. It is used for tiny holes in awkward places, as well as miniature electrical work. To make a hole, you simply turn the tool in your hand. X-acto make one which is available from model shops, or you can order one from the Hobby's catalogue. I recommend getting a pin vice, because you will find it useful in a lot of dolls house work: drilling holes for installing taps (faucets) over sinks, for example, as well as in your normal life, for making pilot holes for cuphooks or for the small screw-eyes that hold the wire for hanging pictures.

Planes and Files

The plane is a simple, old-fashioned smoothing tool that I love using, but it needs constant sharpening. This is done by removing the blade and honing it on a stone, and although the procedure is not overly difficult, I can't really recommend it for a total beginner. Instead, buy the very inexpensive small Surform scraper. This is a tool which works like a cheese grater, paring off unwanted bits of wood, and it will do the job of straightening out any irregular saw cuts. There is a larger version, not unlike a real plane, but the small one is nippy for getting inside window openings.

Another tool which is good for evening out irregularities is an ordinary half-round file. You will find that it also comes in useful for cleaning up any metal accessories that you buy, and for smoothing curves in furniture that you make from wood or card. A rasp is a very coarse file which works the same way but quicker.

Clamps

Sprung clothes pegs make excellent clamps – not too fierce. Stronger are bulldog clips or small alligator clamps, which work on very much the same principle; these can be obtained from most model shops.

Sanders

Plain old sandpaper will do all your sanding jobs for you, but get some fine grades, remembering that the higher the number on the sheet, the finer the grit. For general work, I suggest paper with 100 grit, and for finishing off before painting, the very fine paper known as *"flour paper"*, which has a grit of 200 or 240. An alternative to the coarser paper is a *"sanding block"*, which is a slab of foam covered on four sides with sandpaper of different grades. These come in double combinations: fine/medium for instance.

They can be washed and reused, and their size and shape make them particularly useful for tidying up window holes, and running down the edge of plywood pieces without getting splinters in your fingers.

If you are making a dolls house from scratch, then you might like to hire a power sander along with your jigsaw, but make sure it is an orbital or belt sander, not a sanding disc which will leave circular marks that you can never erase. The sanding sheets supplied by hire firms are coarse compared with ordinary sheets of paper. Use the finest they have, probably a 100 grit, and supplement it with a pack of finishing sheets from a hardware store. English Abrasives sell an excellent pack called Gold: Master Finish, which goes right up to a 320 grade, giving a finish like silk (I use it on full-size furniture too).

For power sanding, lay the pieces of wood flat, and keep the sander working with the grain of the wood, not across it. You will find that you can whip through all the pieces of the dolls house in about half an hour – the power sander is a great time-saver.

A pack of emery boards for filing fingernails will come in handy for small sanding jobs. They are particularly useful because they are firm.

Glues

Recently I treated myself to a hot glue-gun, costing around £10, and it is quite miraculous. The parts bond immediately, and the joint seems very strong. The only disadvantages are the need to move swiftly, and a touch of Melted Cheese Syndrome – trailing wisps of glue that attach themselves in unwanted places.

For normal slow gluing I use Evo-Stick Resin W, a white woodworking glue. It dries nearly transparent, and does not discolour with age, making it useful for other purposes, such as running along the sides of curtains to stop them fraying, or under the edge of fabric carpets for the same purpose. You can buy quicker setting versions of this white glue under many brand names, from model shops. Hobby's UA Woodworking Adhesive (WV 320) is a particularly good one.

I recently read of a clever technique for using the white woodworking glue and the glue-gun together, taking advantage of the best properties of each. You run four-inch long dribbles of Resin W along the edge of the piece to be joined, and make dots with the glue-gun in between. The hot glue from the gun makes an instant bond and holds the join while the slower-acting glue takes effect.

Incidentally, to make it easier to apply the Resin W, decant it into a squeezy bottle with a spout (like a mustard bottle) or use the squeezy bottle that the smaller quantities come in. When I am spreading it over a wide area, I pour some glue into a saucer and apply it with a paint brush. The glue is water-soluble, so it is easy to clean up. I will put a warning in here, though I shall probably repeat it, that all these glues make a barrier that repels stain. It is essential to stain any parts before gluing.

There are occasions when an impact, or contact glue is invaluable for an instant bond, and for this I use Evo-Stick Impact adhesive. It is slightly yellow when dry, so you may prefer a clear adhesive like Bostik All-Purpose. Both of these glues come in tubes, the Evo-stick also in tins for larger quantities.

For sticking down small accessories in the dolls house (pictures on walls, figures on mantelpieces etc.) you can use Blu-tack, a malleable sticky substance. Even better is a clear wax adhesive available from some dolls-house shops (Thames Valley Crafts have it). The other day in a gift shop I found a small tin of "Stick-um" adhesive for holding candles in place, and this works beautifully.

Finally I will list the tools that I consider most useful for dolls-house work, and also the optional extras.

USEFUL TOOLS

mitre box and saw
drill
pin vice
craft knife
geometry set
carpenter's square
Surform scraper
steel rule and ruler
half-round file
junior hacksaw
sandpaper

OPTIONAL EXTRAS

power jigsaw
electric drill
electric sander
Stanley knife
fretsaw
plane

6 · Electrification

When I decided to electrify my own dolls house, the only thing I had ever wired up was a plug, so I had to go and have beginner's lessons with an electrically-minded friend. To my surprise, I found that wiring a dolls house was not at all difficult, and when I flicked the switch for the first time, I was entranced by the change it made. The light gave a warm glow to the rooms, lit up the corners, and made the whole house seem cosy and lived-in. Since that moment, I have never made a house or room that has not been electrified.

In this chapter I will assume that you are about to install lighting in a house that is already built, though ideally not decorated. In theory it is easier to make grooves for wiring or start installing copper tape *before* the house is put together, but in reality this is not very practical. It is hard to decide where to put the lights before you can see the rooms, and it takes a lot of discipline to grind to a halt on construction and go off on another tangent. I prefer to light my houses and rooms after they are built, and in fact, using my preferred system of glueing wires to the ceilings and having wall sockets for lamps on the back wall, you can even decorate most of the house before you start on the wiring.

Normal household current in this country runs on 220 volts. In dolls-house lighting, the current is reduced through a transformer to either 4 or 12 volts. The choice is yours: all the Caroline's Home and Lundby lights run on 4 volts, but most of the lights sold by dolls-house shops are 12 volts. Whatever voltage you choose, the wiring is the same, and a fixture can be changed to another voltage simply by changing the bulb.

I personally do not use the ready-made systems sold by the dolls house firms like Caroline's Home and Lundby. I am sure they work well, but I find them rather confusingly full of plugs and sockets. In my own rooms I have used plain wires, with occasional stretches of copper tape, and I will describe both systems.

ELECTRIFICATION WITH WIRES

The only drawback to this system is that a certain amount of soldering is necessary to connect the wires to the small lampholders, so I will start by telling you how to solder.

Firstly, a soldering iron is more like an iron or a poker than a blow-torch. It won't set fire to the curtains unless you leave it smoldering in the folds, but it will give you a nasty burn if you touch the end. Common sense will tell you to keep the iron safely out of the way when you are not actually using it: I hook mine onto a jar. The idea behind soldering is that you join two things together by means of a "glue" made by melting solder with a touch of the iron. In practice, here is how it works in terms of dolls houses. You need: a **soldering iron** – any size, although a small one is slightly easier to handle – **multi-core solder** – available from any hardware or electrical store – **a vice** – to hold sockets while you solder them.

BULBS AND SOCKETS

In my system I use separate sockets and bulbs which can be unscrewed when they wear out, just like full size ones. If you use the bulbs that are wired up directly (which I admit are smaller and neater), then the whole fitting has to be removed from the ceiling when the bulb fails. Occasionally I do incorporate one of these bulbs, called "grain-of-wheat", into my lighting system, when the fitting I want to use is particularly small and delicate

You can obtain 12-volt bulbs from an electronics shop. Ask them to order T.I.5. LES 12v. 1w. (from RS Components. Cat. no: 587-939). If you are using a 4-volt system (actually 3.5 volt) then you can obtain the bulbs and sockets direct from Hobby's. Sometimes a good model shop will stock them, but be careful that you are not sold 1.5 volt bulbs, which look just the same. Sockets for a 12-volt system will have to come from the same source: Keep the 3.5-volt bulbs for another project.

WIRE

Hobby's sell a beautifully small twin flex, but unfortunately it is brown. You can paint it of course, or buy white single wire, also from Hobby's but rather expensive. Alternatively, go along to your nearest Tandy electrical shop and ask for a 66 ft replacemnt flex for an intercom (called "plug-in connector cord", part no. 43-221). Years ago, some friends gave me a whole reel of this flex from an old baby-alarm that they were no longer using, and I am only just coming to the end of it. It is nearly double the thickness of the wire that comes on bulbs of the Lundby set, but it is a twin flex in an unobtrusive, soft white colour, very flexible and easy to handle.

WIRE STRIPPER

This is an inexpensive tool that you will find invaluable in everyday life: definitely one of my Desert Island Tools. It is available from electrical shops, and looks like a pair of stumpy scissors with a hole between the blades. You can adjust the size of this hole so that it will strip the plastic cover off flex of any size, right down to the very smallest.

Soldering

The first principle of soldering is that everything that is to be joined should be perfectly clean. With a small screwdriver or knife, scrape the brass socket in the two places where wires will be soldered: on its side, and on its end where there is a round brass hole. Put the socket into the vice, so that your two cleaned areas are visible. Take the solder in one hand and the iron in the other, and melt a *very small amount* of solder onto the two clean spots. (The italics are to

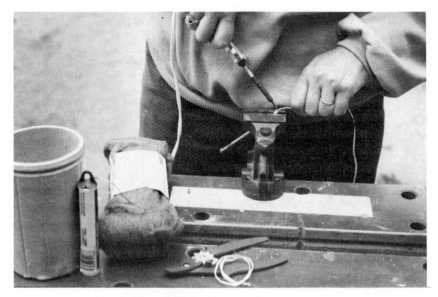

Soldering the wires to a lamp socket

point out another rule of soldering: the less you use the stronger the join.) First step accomplished.

Next step. Take the double flex and split it to a point about 1" up. Cut one side ¼" shorter than the other, then strip the plastic casing off the ends – so that the last ⅛" is bare. Melt a bit of solder onto the tip of the iron, and then wipe the ends of the wires with it: this is known as "tinning" the wires. You now have solder on the wires and on the socket, and all you have to do is use your iron to fuse one to the other. Here is how:

Bend the longer wire out of the way, then place the other wire on the end of the socket – onto that round brass hole that you have previously covered with solder. Touch the tip of the iron to this spot, and you will find that the wire suddenly "pops" in and fuses in place. One word of warning: don't allow too much of the wire to go down into the socket or it will touch the inside wall, and make contact with the other wire, causing the system to short circuit. This happened to my friend Sue who wired up her house rather quickly under Christmas pressure. We spent hours checking the system and trying to discover why the lights were flashing and dimming, and finally had to take the whole thing to my electronics wizard for diagnosis.

The second wire is fused in place in much the same way. Press it onto the bit of solder on the side of the socket, apply the iron until the solder melts, and then hold the wire in place for about two seconds until it hardens again with the wire welded onto the side.

Wiring Overhead Lights

I usually measure the amount of wire I will need for each room: enough to hang down about two inches, go across the ceiling to the back wall, plus about another 18" (46 cm) for connecting at the back. Then I wire a socket for each room and lay them to one side ready for installation.

As you may have gathered from this measuring, my method of wiring a room is fairly primitive. I glue the wire to the ceiling, and then take it out through a little hole drilled in the back wall. The advantages to this system is that the lights are very easy to install, the bulbs are screw-in and can be changed when they fail, and the wires are virtually unnoticeable when papered over or painted to match the ceiling. They are also easy to get at, if something goes wrong with the system. You can conceal the wires totally, if you prefer, by using a saw to make a groove in the floor above (during construction), then the wires can be laid in the groove and fed down into the room below.

The part of my wiring operation that is slightly tricky is the drilling of the holes in the back wall for the wires to pass through. You may have a small drill which can be used inside the dolls house, or find you can hammer a fine nail through the back wall at the point where it joins the ceiling, and then drill the larger hole from the back with an ordinary drill, but if not then this is the time to use your pin vice (see p. 56).

Wall Sockets and Lights

This is the moment to decide where you want to place any wall sockets, and I place them for convenience on the back wall. I drill a hole for the wire to pass through, and then connect it at the back, as I will explain in a moment.

If you want sockets on a side wall, you need a channel to conceal the wire as it makes its way to the back. Borcraft sell a skirting board with a groove to take the flex, and this simplifies the installation of floor sockets, but for a wall sconce you will have to cut a channel with a saw, then cover it with your decoration (internal or external). Alternatively, use the copper tape system described on page 67.

Connecting to Mains

Let us imagine that you now have your lights installed in the house. The wires are glued to the ceilings and are sprouting out of the back of the house. At this point you need a few more things. One is a **transformer** to suit the voltage you have chosen – either 4 or 12 volts. If you have only a few lights (up to ten, including lamps) then you can get away with one of the small transformers with adjustable voltage sold for electronic games. If more, then you must get hold of a large transformer either from a dolls-house shop, or mail order from one of the stockists I have listed at the back of the book. You also need a **connector strip**, available from any electrician, and a short length of fine ordinary light flex.

First you must wire up the connector strip. Look at the next drawing. You will see that the strip consists of pairs of screws (or

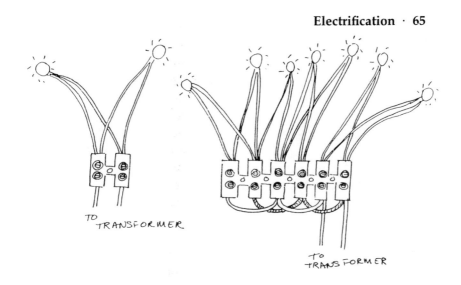

TO TRANSFORMER

TO TRANSFORMER

terminals) which tighten down to hold wires inserted from the sides. The wires from the dolls house go into one side of the block, the wires from the transformer into the other side. If you have only a few wires from the dolls house, you can twist them together and just use one unit of four terminals. Now look at the right-hand drawing. This shows a longer version of the terminal strip, with more holes being activated to take extra wires. So that you don't get muddled when wiring up the new sections of the strip, alternate two different coloured wires from the transformer – blue and brown for instance. When the connector strip is wired up to the transformer, screw it onto the back wall of the house, and you can then join in all the loose wires from the lights into the other side of the strip. Twist several wires together before you insert them into the hole and tighten the screw that hold them. Give a little tug to make sure they are secured. **Warning** make sure that the two wires from a light don't end up going into the same hole, or one that has the same electrical charge – both connecting with a blue flex, for instance. This will cause a short circuit.

There is one other problem that may arise, and that is when one set of wires, possibly from a commercial wall light or socket, turns out to be too short to reach the connector strip. You will need to join in another length of wire, and it is quite straightforward. Cut one of the pair of wires from the light shorter than the other. (This is so that, later, the two spliced joins can't touch each other.) Now

take the new length of wire, separate the two sides of the flex, and cut one of these shorter too, and then strip the plastic casing off the last ½" of all four ends of wire. Twist the wires together to join them, short to long, as in the diagram, and drop a bit of solder on the joints to secure them. If you have staggered the splices as I have described, there is no need to insulate the bare wires, but if they are touching, you must cover them with insulating tape or with some of the silicone sealer sold for filling gaps between bathtub and wall.

When you have all the wires from the dolls house joined into the connector block, which in turn is wired to the transformer, you can finally plug the latter into the wall. You should have total illumination inside your house. But what if you don't?

Possible Faults:

NOTHING LIGHTS UP AT ALL

You probably have a loose connection. Give a little pull on all the wires where they join the connector strip and make sure they are secured. Take out the flexes and see if you need to strip a bit more off the ends of the wires. If the plastic insulation goes into the connector strip it may prevent a good contact inside.

ONE OR TWO LIGHTS DON'T LIGHT UP

Follow these out through the back of the house and check their connections. Have a look at the socket: one of the wires may have been weakly soldered and have come undone. You may be able to solder it in situ, but often it is easier to pull the wire out and hold it in the vice to resolder it. A touch with the iron should connect it again. You may have a dud bulb. Try it in a socket that works.

A bulb will not light if it is not screwed in far enough to reach the back of the socket. Hold it in one hand and screw the bulb in tightly with the other. Have you distorted the socket by squeezing it too tightly in the vice?

ALL THE LIGHTS ARE DIM AND FLUTTERING

The system is shorting. This means that somewhere along the line, two bare wires from the same light are touching or making contact with each other. You may have stripped too much plastic off the flex above the connector strip or above one of the sockets. Read p. 63.

If you are stumped, you may be able to locate a fault by pulling the wires of the transformer out of the connector strip and touching its two leads to various points of contact along the way.

COPPER TAPE

I used this as a complete system for the first time the other day when a friend brought her house over to electrify. I had tried the copper tape previously for short connections in awkward places, and was not totally enamoured of it, but since Alli had bought a whole reel of tape we decided to use it.

First step was to measure the distance from the middle of each room to the back of the house, and cut some lengths of tape to fit. Each light needs two tapes, corresponding to the two wires of the other system. Laying the house on its back, we peeled the backing off the tape and began to stick it to the ceilings in rather wavering lines, ⅛" apart, and overlapping about ½" onto the back wall. This ½" was our magical connecting place, and into it we had to insert two tiny brass nails. These would then protrude through the back wall, so that we could connect them to the main wiring system behind, which would be much the same as on a conventionally wired house.

Alli's dolls house consists of four main rooms and two attic bedrooms. Two of the main rooms contain staircases and are about 14" wide: getting our arms, hammer and tiny tacks into these was testing, but not beyond our ability. The other two rooms, however, were the same depth (15"), but much narrower, and trying to hammer inside this confined space with nails the size of ¼" dressmaking pins provoked imprecations from us both. Finally I decided that we should use my pin vice and drill tiny holes through the tape. Alli didn't find this particularly easy either, and I heard her muttering about "visit to the oculist", but at last we had our brass pins sticking out of the back of the house. Onto each of these we twisted a length of wire, bent the nails over with pliers, and then dropped a blob of solder onto the join to hold it. These wires went into a connector strip as before.

The actual lights were fitted with two tiny wires, and these were to be connected to the tape system with some special little plugs and sockets supplied by the same shop. The sockets had minute brass nails that had to be placed so that one pierced each of the copper strips taped to the ceiling. Then the wires from the light fixtures were threaded through the little plugs, following the instructions that accompanied them, and with the house resting on its roof, we (or rather I) managed to attach the little plugs, first pressing them into place with my fingers, then hammering them home with a small tack hammer. In retrospect, I think most of these operations would have been made easier if we had first made small pilot holes with a hatpin (and indeed the firm now offers a special hole-making tool.)

When we had the whole house wired up, we plugged in the transformer and went triumphantly round to the front: nothing. After a lot of fiddling around, and by dint of detaching the transformer leads and applying them to various sections of the copper tape, we realized that the holes we had drilled through to the back were too big, so that the brass nails were not making a good contact with the tape. We remedied this by replacing the ceiling strips and repiercing them with the nails. This time everything worked.

The major advantage to this system is that the copper tape is flat and can be papered over, although the outline remains faintly visible. Complicated wiring systems, incorporating many sockets and wall lights can be installed before the decoration is done, and new lights can easily be added. The drawback is that every junction where two tapes cross must be pinned with the little nails in order to maintain the electrical current, and if these nails loosen, the contact is lost.

In all wiring systems, it is easiest to take the wires straight out to the back wall for connection outside. Then the only wire visible inside the house is on the ceilings – barely noticeable. When it comes to wiring a house that is open at the back, like so many of the American ones, the wires have to run down the side walls instead, and this gives an advantage to the flat tape system.

LIGHT FITTINGS

Many beautiful fittings are available from dolls-house shops, some hand-made and very expensive, others designed for the mass-produced children's houses. These lamps are often fitted with grain-of-wheat bulbs and to convert a 4-volt lamp to a 12 or vice versa, simply pull the bulb and its wires out and thread one of the other voltage in. The soldered sockets with separate bulbs are sometimes too bulky, but you can use the grain-of-wheat ones instead.

To make inexpensive overhead lights, buy some ping pong balls. For a globe light, leave them whole, make a hole in one end big

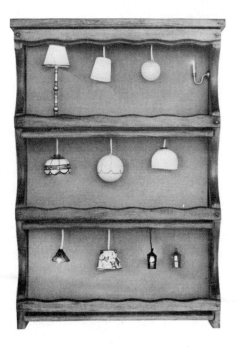

Lights: commercial, improvised and
home-made

enough to take the bulb and socket, and cover the hole with a glued-on scrap of card or paper after it is wired up. You can also make two slits in the form of a cross and push the bulb and socket through but it is difficult to get them back out to change the bulb. For a neat finish, cover the hole with a brass no. 4 screw cup washer; I use these on all my ping pong ball shades.

A simple shade, which is effective in a kitchen or office, is made by cutting the ping pong ball in half (with a craft knife) along the seamline and using both halves. In art supply shops you can buy a plastic sheet of templates for various sizes of circle. Lay one of these over your ping pong ball, and using the circle marked 1⅜" (or 36 mm) draw a pencilled ring around the ball (this will be about ¼" above the seam line). To make a Tiffany-style shade (middle row in photo), use the quartered markings on the template to divide the pencil line into even sections. Split the ping pong ball with a craft knife and, taking the larger piece, cut a scalloped edge with nail scissors, using the pencilled markings as a guide. Put the shade on a table and, looking down on it, pierce a hole for the flex to go through. Now you can paint the shade with permanent markers, acrylic paints, nail varnish, or whatever you find easiest to use, dividing the sections with black lines, drawn with an overhead projector pen from an artist's supply shop. To make more parallel rings, lay the template over the shade again. If you are not artistic, just divide the shade up at random, like a crazy quilt. If you are handy with pens or brushes, paint designs on: garlands of grapes, flowers and leaves.

My own favourite shade starts with the same cut ping pong ball as in the Tiffany shade, without the scalloped edge. I use the finest silk I can get hold of (lining silk, for instance, or some parachute silk that I was once given) to cover the ball, sticking it with white glue (do *not* use Copydex or any other latex glue that might yellow with age). To make the silk fit over the curves I snip it and overlap, or cut out triangular wedges as I go along. Then round the bottom edge I glue some very fine lace or fringe. I usually have a supply of this gleaned from hours of hovering over lace counters and looking through baskets of oddments in antique shops and markets.

N.B. It is important, when covering or painting these shades, not to use a heavy fabric or dense paint which will obscure the light. The ping pong balls are already slightly opaque, and you may end

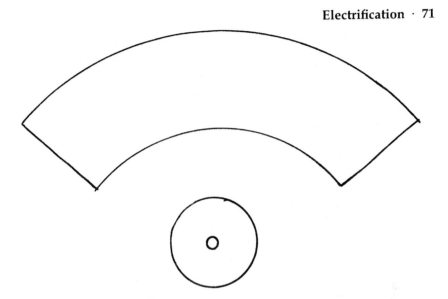

up with no light coming through the shade.

I have made another successful shade of parchment coloured writing paper, oiled to make it translucent (photo p. 69: bottom row). I drew the shape shown in the diagram above, then painted a design on it and cut it out. The top edge I glued round a piece of card that had a hole cut in it for the flex. Many variations on this shade could be devised, some with scalloped edges, some made out of lace stiffened with wallpaper paste, or stuck onto greaseproof or waxed paper.

Here are some other ideas for shades:

- Buy one of the gold or silver bells sold for wedding cakes and scrape the paint off.
- A small basket with the handle removed.
- Fluted paper cases sold for sweets are available in plain colours from specialist kitchen shops.
- For a tiny shade, use a bowl or cup from a plastic tea set. The handle is easily nipped off with a craft knife.

Lanterns sold as Christmas tree lights or decorations can be painted and used outside the front door (photo: bottom right). To wire them up, use copper tape running behind the door of the house into the hinge, linking up with more copper tape on the side

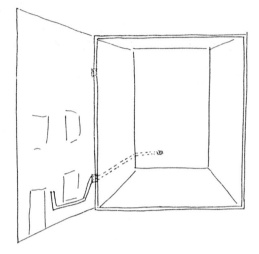

wall and leading out to the back. The hinge will act as contact point between the two lengths of copper tape.

Lamps

In my section of lighting suppliers at the back of the book you will find several stockists of lamps. You can also concoct lamp bases from beads threaded on brass tubing, or stacked and glued together, or from empty cotton reels. A disc of card around the bulb will hold the shade in place.

I rarely try to make wall brackets because the commercial ones are so much better than my efforts. In the photograph on p. 69 you can see a single candle sconce which costs £5 from Wood 'n' Wool Miniatures. The stained glass shade on the bottom left costs £1.50 from Wentways Miniatures.

In case you have read this chapter with scepticism and are still thinking that electricity is too dangerous to work with, let me point out that standard domestic 220 voltage is a very different thing from 4 or 12 volts. Even if you touch the bare wires inside your dolls house the current will be imperceptible.

7 · Two Houses Made from Kits

By a stroke of luck, two of my friends had decided to make dolls houses from kits just when I wanted to write about it. Felicity had chosen a Georgian manor made by Honeychurch, and sold to her through a retail shop. Sally had ordered one from a mail order firm (the Dolls House Emporium), through a catalogue. They were similar in style, both having the vaguely Georgian facade much favoured by dolls-house builders. We started both kits on the same day.

Stage one: We Open the Boxes

Felicity's Honeychurch kit was larger and heavier than the other, which was to be expected, since her kit had cost exactly double (£120). When opened, we found her box contained a great number of wooden pieces large and small, all in birch plywood of the highest quality, beautifully finished. There was no parts list so, using the assembly diagrams as a guide, we began by sorting the small bits into bags labelled "portico", "upper windows, bars, surround and sill" etc., and eventually all the mysterious pieces found homes. In the course of the sorting we worked out how to assemble all the components except the staircase, which looked very daunting indeed, having half landings on each floor. We also pushed the walls of the house roughly together (laying it on its back) to get an idea of the size of the rooms.

Sally's wood was lower grade plywood, but adequate for the purpose, I thought, assuming that one would be painting it. It was clearly going to need a lot of sanding before assembly. The windows were ready-made all-in-one with their surrounds, out of plastic, so there were far fewer pieces of trim to sort. The instructions were good, and a parts list was given which we found very useful. We slotted this house together too, and found a few small disappointments. There were no hallways, because the stairs were enclosed on both sides, and went straight up without

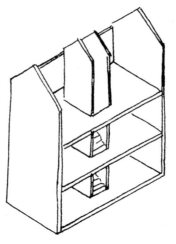

landings. This did not leave enough room for doors between rooms, and instead there were simply gaps at front and back of the centre partition (drawing). The top floor (of three) was only six inches high (15 cm) at the front edge, so the roof space was utilized to give height to the rooms. This made attractive atticky shaped rooms with eaves, but meant that the roof could not be used for extra bedrooms.

Stage two: We Modify the Kits

Felicity and I decided at once that even though she already had three floors in her house, we would open out the roof space for attic bedrooms. (There never seem to be enough rooms in a dolls house.) We measured the height of the triangular roof ends, and found that only 5½" (13.5 cm) had been allowed. We knew from my dolls house that 6" (15 cm) was a bare minimum, so we decided to prop the whole roof up with strips of wood, behind the existing parapet.

We knew that in both houses we wanted windows in the side walls, in all the rooms. Otherwise, once the front of the house is opened, there are no windows to curtain and decorate around – just empty boxes. For Felicity's house, we copied the size of the top storey front windows, enlarging it slightly for the ground floor. We didn't want the windows to be too big, otherwise they would take up too much space in the room.

No glazing is suppled for the Honeychurch house, because the makers feel that children could poke it out. Since there was space behind the glazing bars, however, we decided to add some sheet acrylic later – as a dust preventative and to add realism.

Quite a few changes were planned for Sally's house. She was desperate for at least a small bit of hallway, having fallen in love with an umbrella stand in my dolls house, so we took one of the upright partitions that enclose the stairs, and cut a piece off it, the height of the bottom storey. Then we cut a new wall of the same height out of a piece of plywood, but moved it over a bit to divide the space into a hallway and dining room (see photo on p. 76). In this wall we cut a hole for a door. For the two rooms on the top floor, the ones with the atticky ceilings, we also cut two more partitions, so that each could be divided in half, making up for the lack of bedrooms in the roof. Obviously one of these rooms on each side would have to be very narrow, but at least she could have a bathroom, and perhaps a tiny baby's room. Sally then started marking out her extra windows in the side walls. The same plastic windows (actually quite nice) as the ones supplied with the kit, are available in three sizes separately, from the catalogue, so we designed the new openings to fit them. The surrounds of these windows would cover any flaws in the cutting.

Stage three: Using Power Tools

I had decided that I would make Sally and Felicity do all the work on the houses to get a true picture of any difficulties, confining myself to hovering over them with advice. Sally's first bad moment came when she had to learn to use the power jigsaw. I let her start on a piece of scrap wood, explaining the rules that I have set out in chapter 5, and after sawing only about two inches she said, "Right, I see," and set off on her window holes and doorways. She handled the straight cuts beautifully with little waver, and only took a bit of time learning to make corners (we had one or two arches that had to be straightened out). After a while she commented that it was like learning to use an electric sewing machine, a bit nerve-wracking to begin with, but pretty straight-forward after a little practice.

Felicity found the straight cuts easy too, but couldn't master my patent cornering system (p. 53), so we ended up drilling holes in each corner of the window area, and after that she was fine. Neither she nor Sally really liked using the saw, partly because it was unfamiliar, partly because of the noise and vibration, but they both managed it, and I don't think they would have much enjoyed using a keyhole saw either, which is the only alternative for cutting windows.

The dolls' house kits, open

As we were working on Sally's house, we suddenly had the inspiration to add a shop onto the side. The ground floor side window we immediately cut down to the floor to convert it to an arched doorway, and we took a tea-break while we drew up some plans. A sketch of the proposed inside and outside first, then an examination of the ceiling and window heights in the house itself, to determine how tall the shop could/should be. Since we were adding on a shop, why not a store-room overhead? We decided on an overall height of 18" (46 cm), which would bring the apex of the storeroom roof just under the top storey window sill. Access to the shop from the main house would be through the archway we had already cut, and on the store-room level, through a cupboard-sized door made out of the window hole on the first floor level. We wanted maximum ceiling height in the shop, so we brought the ceiling right up under the first floor windows – giving us nearly two inches more than the bottom storey of the house. This left us with 7½" (19 cm) overall height for the storeroom.

We made a cutting plan next, to determine how much wood we would need: the base, sides and front out of ⅜" (1 cm) plywood, the roof and internal partitions of ¼" (6 mm). No stairs, but possibly a ladder into the store-room, which could double as a small bedroom if need be. All the pieces of the shop would be cut out at our next session.

Stage four: We Assemble the Shells

Felicity decided to put her stairs together before assembling the house, but Sally's stairs depended on adjustment of the steps after the shell of the house had been built. The Honeychurch instructions were fine on the stairs, although we spent a long time looking for some triangular shaped pieces that were taped together so that they looked square. This type of confusion could have been avoided with a list of parts.

Felicity wanted her stairs warm brown and, knowing that wood glue repels stain, we wiped all the parts over with Blackfriars Teak Wood Dye before starting the assembly. Then she took them home to glue together, to save time at our next work session. When she returned with them, it transpired that she had not read the instruction that said, "Glue the steps onto the baseboards, *spacing them evenly to reach each end*" (my italics). Instead, she had crammed as many on as would fit, leaving us short of treads for the fourth baseboard, and with steps projecting slightly out over the ends of the three that she had finished. As everything was well and truly glued together, we pared the projections down with a knife, and I cut her two more steps from some triangular moulding of the right size, which I had just bought for the house I was making myself. She had glued the banisters together correctly, following the full-size pattern given in the instructions, and we glued them to the steps. Assembly of the whole staircase we thankfully left till the next session, and turned to fitting the glazing bars to the windows. These were already glued together, but needed to be pared down with a knife to fit the window holes. We were beginning to understand why ready-made houses command such high prices.

Sally meanwhile, with her much simpler kit, was ready to put the shell together. We followed the instructions to the letter, using masking tape occasionally to hold pieces together, and in no time at all had the frame assembled. Here again the stairs were tricky: a much simpler design than the Honeychurch ones, but the assembly had to be done inside the house, with nothing to support the stairs except one side wall. We cheated and used my hot glue-gun, which sets immediately, but an alternative would be to mark the position of the stairway on the side wall, and then use an impact glue to ensure an immediate bond. Even with this complication, we found the house quick and fun to put together, and soon reached the stage of putting in the extra walls for the hall and the attic rooms.

At this point we realised that the house was very slightly too small. The ceiling height of the two bottom stories is only just over 8″ (20 cms), and the internal dimensions of the rooms, 11½″ deep (29 cms) by 10″ wide (25 cm), hardly enough to take the extra walls we had optimistically planned. Still, we decided to go ahead, but to make the right-hand partition on the top floor only come part of the way into the room, leaving an L-shaped space around it. You can see this in the photo.

Felicity now completed her stairs. The instructions were clear, but we still made a lot of stupid mistakes, gluing the wrong pieces together and having to prise them apart. When finished they looked beautiful, and worth the fuss. Next we turned to the assembly of the house. Again this was straightforward and fun, and the one change we made was in leaving the insertion of the stairs until a later date. The instructions were to nail the internal walls to the sides of the staircases before slotting them in, but this looked difficult, and anyway we wanted to paint the shell with the staircases out, to avoid getting paint on the stained wood. We left the back off, and tried the stairs to make sure there were no fatal flaws, but in fact they were such a lovely snug fit that I think I would recommend fitting them as we did. Another point is that once they were installed in the finished house, it would clearly be quite impossible to stick down a stair carpet on the return flights of stairs, which are really only visible from the back.

In assembling the shell, gluing and nailing where instructed, we only twice had to remove nails that we hammered in sideways so that they made an unwanted entry into one of the rooms (we pushed them back out with the blade of a screwdriver). We then stuck the top piece of the pediment onto the front of the house. Now we realized that the front of the roof could not be hinged, as we had planned, because it couldn't swing past the pediment. Instead, the whole roof would have to lift off, the chimneys serving as handles.

We added a partition in one of the upstairs rooms to make a bathroom, leaving an L-shaped room around it, as we had done in Sally's house, and we also cut a hole in the top-storey hall ceiling for a ladder to the roof.

Stage five: Finishing the Houses

The side window holes of both houses were now tidied up with a file, and we all agreed that they were worth the extra trouble. With the shells assembled, there was a lovely fall of light through these windows that gave us an excited feeling of anticipation about the furnishing and decoration. After all the hours of work, suddenly these were *real* dolls houses, and we could begin to talk about exterior paint colours, wallpapers for the inside walls, and the dolls house fair in Birmingham on Sunday, to which we were all three making an expedition.

But there was still some work to be done. Both houses were given a preliminary coat of white household emulsion, inside and out. This was lightly sanded, then the ceilings were given another coat, while the fronts of the houses were painted in their final colours: Laura Ashley "stone" for Sally, soft green for Felicity. All trim would be a gentle white, in silk finish for a soft sheen.

When Sally came to paint the stairwell we very much regretted that she hadn't done this before assembling the shell. There was barely room to wield the brush inside the narrow space. Had we realized this, we would probably have painted and papered the halls before putting them in. We also felt that the stairs were looking a bit crude, so they were painted with yellow ochre paint, then walnut-coloured varnish stain, a technique described more fully on p. 25. The trim for the fronts of both houses was sanded and painted before being stuck on, and Sally's plastic windows were taken outside and sprayed with a can of white car primer, to take away the plastic shine. They look superb. A last touch was to add a plinth, made of strips of wood, to the bottom of the house and shop, so that the doors could open easily.

The final bits of trim were added to the facade of the Honeychurch house, but we got very confused when assembling the porch, worrying over phrases like "glue the thin strips to the porch apex and porch block". In retrospect, of course, it's easy to see what they meant, but none of the parts is labelled in the drawing: a good example of instructions written by someone to whom the construction is already obvious. Still, we managed it in the end with the last unclaimed strip of wood finally slotting in as the door jamb for the front door.

The dolls-house kits, shut

There is a photograph of the finished houses so you can decide for yourself which you prefer. I myself think the one from the Dolls House Emporium has the more interesting and imaginative facade, but there is slightly more room in the Honeychurch house, and it certainly has a better staircase. The quality of the plywood in the Honeychurch house is much higher than in Sally's kit, but I wonder how important this is if the house is to be painted anyway. Apparently some people prefer to varnish the natural wood, but I feel that this makes the house look more like a cupboard than a dolls house.

There are several other kits on the market, and many of them can be seen already constructed in dolls-house shops. Wansbeck Hobbies have a line of beautiful Norfolk houses which are available as kits, and Minimus in Cambridge have Jane Charlotte houses and shops, and also the range of American kits by Greenleaf. These are typically American, and open from the back, but they are full of interesting detail and quirks, and might be a good choice for anyone who,is jaded with Georgian dolls-house elegance. They range from a charming Victorian cottage with a porch and lots of gingerbread trim for £35, to a big Tudor mansion at £120, with moveable partitions so you can design your own rooms. There is also a dear little Cottage Shop, with bay windows and a loft overhead. These houses are not expensive, in spite of being imported, but the thin plywood construction makes them unsuitable for very young children, and they need a lot of care in the finishing. They look marvellous when well sanded and painted, but pretty tacky if left so that the slot assembly is visible.

Before you start of any kit, examine all the parts carefully, and read the instructions right through. Don't feel that the construction you are given is solemn and binding: it is your house now, and you are free to alter it as you wish, providing that you don't remove some crucial structural wall. Change the outside trim, if you like, and look around at real houses for ideas on painting the exterior. Add internal doors, chimney breasts, or any other missing features, using the instructions in chapters 9 and 10.

And finally, the moral of this chapter is: don't start your kit on Christmas Eve.

8 · My Dolls Houses

My first real dolls house was made out of a cupboard that I found at an auction. It was quite a good size, 3' tall (90 cm), including a 6" (15 cm) plinth at the bottom. There were two shelves, giving three stories, each 9½ to 10" (25 cm) high – just about right for a dolls house room. However, as I began to plan the internal divisions, I realized that the house was going to be too narrow (23", 58 cm) to have a hallway and two rooms on each floor, and that I would have to have the stairway in one of the rooms. In theory this should present no problem. As long as the room is wide enough, there should be room for the furniture, but in practice you are left with only two usable walls. You can fill in the space under the stairs to make another wall, but the room still tends to be deep and narrow,

My dolls house made from a cupboard

with an irretrievably hall-like effect. In time I became so annoyed by this that I built on an extension to my house, giving me a kitchen, extra bedroom and roof garden, as seen in the photograph. The hallways have become features. They are much wider than I would ever have made them if I had been building the house from scratch, and I have room for a hat stand and a piano, and even managed to cram a tiny bathroom into the corner of one hall, without having to sacrifice a precious bedroom.

This cupboard was an ideal way for me to start. I had very few tools and fewer skills, and I was too scared to start with a sheet of plywood. My difficulties were in cutting the windows and the holes for the stairwell. The shelves and sides of the cupboard were of very thin plywood (⅛", 3 mm) fastened to a timber framework.

My dolls house, open

They were somewhat worm-eaten, and inclined to splinter and disintegrate when cut with a key-hole saw, so I borrowed a power jigsaw and used that instead. I had to remove the shelves in order to cut the stairwells. All my holes were pretty wobbly and not very clean-cut because I was using the wrong sort of blade (see p. 53 for blades), but there they were, and the cupboard was now beginning to take on a distinctly dolls-housey air. I found that the rooms already had an individual atmosphere due to the age of the cupboard, and to the recesses and protrusions made by the shelf supports and timber framing.

The depth of the cupboard (13″, 33 cm) was perfect on the top storey at eye level, but a bit deep on the ground floor. I decided to put a false wall across the back of the two bottom rooms, and cut an archway in one of them, which was to be the dining room. You can see the archway with a little table behind it, in the photograph. I like the feeling that there is a corridor outside, leading to some invisible part of the house.

The dining room in my cupboard house

It took me a long, long time to finish the house, and I got extremely bored with the windows – all those little glued-on sticks for glazing bars. The extension, on the other hand, was finished in a couple of weeks, working on and off. I was more skilful by the time I tackled it, and it was a much smaller unit. Since that time I have found myself concentrating more on miniature rooms, but I find myself drawn back now to the larger conception, and have just begun a new project, which I shall describe.

MAKING A HOUSE FROM SCRATCH

After years of trying to whip up enthusiasm in my first two children, now aged 18 and 19, I finally had to admit that they were never going to play with dolls houses. Marguerite had some happy times with the Sindy house I made her, and Daniel toyed with a train set, mainly to please his grandfather, but it wasn't till Eleanor came along that I saw a ray of hope.

By the time she was seven or eight, she had begun to ask if she could play with my dolls house. To tell the truth, I don't really like people rearranging my house – I have such a clear idea of where things go – but Eleanor played quite nicely with it until the day she and her friend decided to have a burglary. The resulting chaos threw me into a rage that effectively killed their fun, although I suppose I should have been thankful they weren't playing Earthquakes like some children I heard of. She lost interest for a while, and then began watching me as I worked on my half-scale house (see p. 98), asking periodically if it could be hers. Finally she said, "Mummy, would you make *me* a dolls house?"

It quickly transpired that she had some strong ideas of what she would like: a semi-detached ("So the children can go next door to play," she said, her eyes shining), one side having a shop downstairs. I made a rough sketch of the interior of the half that was to have the shop, with some indication of dimensions. Obviously, unless the whole thing was to be a monster, dominating her room, the two semi-detached halves would have to be pared down to the minimum. I finally decided on the plan on pp. 86 and 87. The right-hand side has the shop on the ground floor, and a hallway with the stairs going across the back to allow maximum width to the room, and foreshorten it. The same principle applies upstairs, where the kitchen again has stairs at the back, while the partition wall moves a bit to the right to divide the floor almost equally. Next floor has three small rooms, one of them a hallway, and finally, a ladder will lead up to the attic bedrooms overhead.

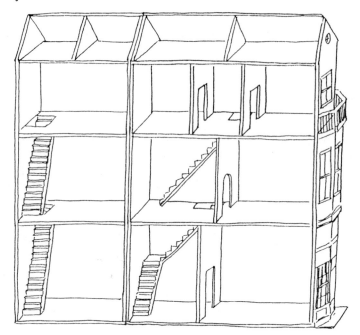

The other side of the house, which is roughly the same width as the shop alone (15", 38 cm), has the stairs going right up through the rooms, because Eleanor wanted it that way. I have had to ignore my own rule of keeping the stairs separate, because there simply wasn't room.

Eleanor had a picture of how she wanted the front of the house, with one section projecting forward with a gable roof. The shop door and display windows we decided to put on the side of the house, so that it could be played with when the main doors of the house were open. As you will see, in the course of drawing the exterior, various small details were added as they occurred to me.

Now I made a fresh drawing of my house plans, marking in the dimensions more clearly, and labelling the walls. Next I put them in groups according to size, as shown on p. 88, then I drew the outlines of 2 sheets of 8' by 4' (120 cm by 240 cm) plywood, so I could lay out the pieces. This is my system for all sorts of woodworking projects. I rarely make scale drawings, although I do try to keep the proportions more or less accurate by eye.

One sheet of ⅜" (1 cm) plywood did for the main walls and the

base (see diagram), and one of ¼" (6 mm) for back, roofs and internal partitions. I made the two sides of the house detachable, so they could be moved away from each other for play. The cost of the plywood was £28.

Once the plywood had been delivered, I marked it out, checking all the dimensions again, and making sure I had allowed for wall thicknesses. This is why I like the three-dimensional drawing – you can actually *see* which walls overlap each other. I cut the wood with my power jigsaw (see p. 53), then sanded it all with a power sander.

Windows

Now came the moment to decide on the windows, because I wanted to cut them next. I remembered with dread the hours spent on glazing bars for my cupboard house, and toyed with the idea of buying ready-made windows. Wooden ones are a terrible price, and would add too much to the cost of the house because I needed so many. The Dolls House Emporium sells the plastic windows which they supply with their kits, but I knew that they were too

Front:	28″ × 14¾″	A^1	× 2
	28″ × 8″	A^2	× 1
	28″ × 2″	A^3	× 2
Sides:	34½″ × 13″	B	× 4
Interior walls:	13″ × 9″	C^1	× 3
	13″ × 10½″	C^2	× 1
Roofs:	10″ × 14¾″	D^1	× 2
	10″ × 22¾″	D^2	× 2
Backs:	28″ × 14¾″	E^1	× 1
	28″ × 22¾″	E^2	× 1
Floors:	14″ × 13″	F^1	× 3
	22″ × 13″	F^2	× 3
Base:	14¾″ × 13″	X^1	× 1
	24″ × 13″	X^2	× 1

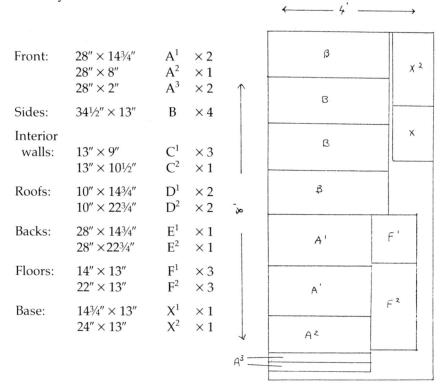

grand for this style of house. I wanted an Edwardian window, tall and narrow, not fat and impressive in the high Georgian style. A conversation with Mr Wooi of Wentways Miniatures yielded the offer of a really simple wooden window kit, priced at under £2. The principle on which it is based could be copied by anyone with a mitre box and saw (p. 56). The surround of the window is made of L-shaped moulding, with both sides ⅜″ wide (it is called "corner angle" and is sold by Jennifers of Walsall and Borcraft Miniatures). One edge of the moulding covers the cut edge of the window hole, and the other makes the surround, with the corners mitred. In the kit, the glazing bars are made of two strips of wood which snap together across each other, but the same effect could be had by gluing one strip upright, then having two short strips on each side. As a guide for getting these correctly in position, slip a piece of graph paper under the window hole that you are working on. Better still, make the lines that you are following on the graph paper even darker with a felt-tip marker.

For glazing the windows, sheet acetate can be obtained from almost any dolls house or model shop, and is easily cut with scissors. Glue it to the back of the glazing bars. I should mention here, that you should finish all the wallpapering before installing any windows, because it is easier to cut out the paper over the window and door spaces from outside the room with a knife (p. 108).

Assembly

The house is assembled like an open box. First the top and bottom are nailed onto the two sides, then the back goes on and holds the four sides squarely in position. To support the internal shelves (floors), I glue strips of cove or cornice moulding to the sides and back of the house, and it also serves as a decorative feature in the rooms. These shelves can be slotted in without glue, while you plan the layout of the stairs. The wall partitions between rooms will simply be glued in after cutting out any doorways. I rely on the glue, and the skirting boards which will come later, to hold the walls in place.

Stairs

The design of the stairs will depend on the height of the room. They can go straight up in one flight, or have a half landing, which is tricky to construct but looks marvellous. For a comparison of the two types of stairs, look at the pictures of the kits we made on page 76. A simple way to make stairs, and the one I always use, is to glue short lengths of ¾" (2 cm) triangular moulding onto a thin plywood base. You can see what I mean more clearly by looking at the photograph of my hall on page 90, especially if you look at the short flight beside the bathroom. In a 10" (25 cm) high room you will need fifteen steps, and a length of wood about 12½" long (32 cm) to glue them to. You can space the steps out a bit if they don't quite reach the landing.

The banisters in my cupboard house are pretty crude: just pieces of dowelling glued to the stairs and to the rail. It drove me mad trying to put them in, with the top of the dowels slipping just as I got the bottoms glued in place. Nowadays you can buy a special handrail with a groove on the underside which holds the banisters.

The hall in my cupboard house

If you want to secure the bottom of the banisters as well, you can make thin treads to go on the top of each step out of strips of wood ½" wide (12 mm) and 1/16" thick (1.5 mm). Tape these all together with masking tape, then drill a small hole through the whole lot, right near the edge, where the banister will go. When one of these strips is glued to each step, you will have a neat little hole for the bottom of the banister.

If this all sounds too much, you might like to invest in a stairway kit. The Mulberry Bush have a wooden one, and you can choose between a straight flight, or one with a turn and a half landing. For real economy, Hobby's sell a plastic stairway which is moulded all in one. It's only long enough for a 6" high ceiling (15 cm), but with ingenuity, two of them could be cut and arranged with a half landing. The sides are solid, but could be improved by the addition of a handrail and some panelling, then the whole painted to conceal the plastic.

When cutting the hole for the stairwell, remember that you need to leave a small section at the top of the stairs to serve as a landing.

Doors

I have an easy and inexpensive system for making panelled doors. I have given the template (sized for 1/12 scale houses), for a rather grand Georgian door (p. 92). It can be adapted to make a humbler door which would suit a kitchen or attic in a formal house, by following the dotted lines. I recommend making a template out of thin card before you start, then you will have firm edges to draw round on subsequent copies. To make a template, trace or photocopy the pattern, then paste this copy onto some light card. Using a ruler and craft knife, cut right through the paper and card along the marked lines, so that the shaded areas are removed. To use this template, lay it over some firmer card (ask for "four sheet" card, it's a bit lighter than picture mounting board). Draw round all the panels and the outside edge, then use your knife and ruler again to cut out the shaded areas. Make two copies from card, one for each side of the door, then cut a piece of 3/16" or ¼" (5 mm) plywood, using the outer edge of the template only, so that no panels are removed. One piece of card is glued to each side of the plywood, and there you have a panelled door. With practice, using a sharp craft knife you will find that you will be able to angle the blade slightly to give a bevelled edge to your panels. When these doors are well sanded and given a couple of coats of paint (and see p. 125 for simulated wood finish), they look virtually indistinguishable from ones made up laboriously with strips of wood. However, if you want a plain wood door, or wish to expend a bit more labour on an imposing front door, then you can use my template as a guide for laying on strips of wood bought from a model shop.

Doors can be hung with real miniature hinges, but in my experience they tend to get ripped off in play. If you do use them, they are easier to install before you have inserted the partition walls into the house. Also, I recommend that you glue a tiny strip of wood to the floor to act as a doorstop, to stop people forcing the doors the wrong way.

The doors in my dolls house have been hung on little pins at top and bottom, and I will describe my method. You need a pin vice (a

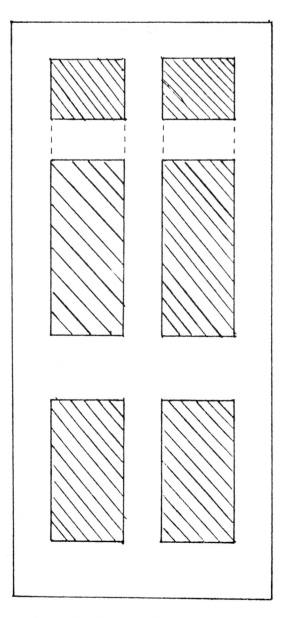

small drilling tool described on p. 56), and some ½" panel pins (tiny nails with hardly any head). In the top and bottom of the door, about ⅛" (2.5 mm) from the end, drill holes ¼" deep to take the panel pins. In the top of the doorway, 3/16th of an inch from the

corner edge, drill another small hole, big enough so that a panel pin can turn freely in it. For the bottom pin fixing, I recommend cutting a narrow piece of wood to serve as a threshold. Then the bottom panel pin can be inserted up through this piece of wood and into the door, *before* it is inserted into the doorway. Look at the drawing for more clarity. This threshold piece will allow the door to clear any carpets that you might be installing later.

Roof

The simplest kind of roof is a roof garden. Next is a simple pitched roof, like the one drawn on p. 94. When cutting out the house, make the sides longer and pointed at the top to support the roof. You will find it infinitely easier to fit the two halves of the roof, if the pointed apex of the sides is a perfect right-angle. If it isn't, then where the edges of the roof meet at the top, they will have to be pared away slightly to make a snug fit. Most difficult of all is the sort of pitched roof that I have on my dolls house where all the bits of the roof meet at different angles. When I made it, I just trimmed the edges in a hit or miss way until they went together neatly.

If you have a roof, then you might as well use it for attic bedrooms. Cut the front half of the roof into two pieces (look at p. 94 again), and glue the narrow top strip in place. The lower half of the roof is hinged so that it lifts up to allow you to get at the attic. To

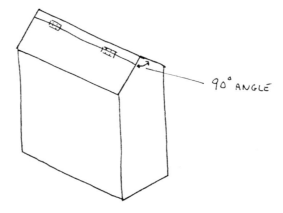

make a partition wall, take a stiff piece of paper and fold the edges in until it fits in neatly. Use this as a template and draw round it on a piece of plywood. You will find that there is not enough height in this wall to allow for a proper doorway, so just cut a small hole or archway of some sort. Attics often have cramped little doors anyway.

Finishing the Roof

A coat of dark paint often looks very effective as a finish for a roof, especially if the colour is chosen to blend with the rest of the exterior. Roof papers imitating red or green tiles and grey slates can be bought from most dolls-house or model shops, and they are easy to apply with wallpaper paste. For something more realistic, cut slates from card or thin wood – either individually or in long strips, with slits to indicate the edge of each tile. Starting at the lower edge of the roof, glue these in place, overlapping the rows and staggering the joins like brickwork (contact glue is easiest here). If using card, then paint the whole roof in a soft grey, and pick out individual slates with variations in colour. Wood can be given the same treatment, or stained instead, for a shingled effect.

Real wood shingles are available in packets from some dolls house suppliers, and although they look overwhelming when viewed in heaps on the table, they are actually surprisingly quick to apply. I shingled the entire roof of my half-scale house in an afternoon. To stain these shingles, shake them in a jar half-filled with diluted wood dye (medium or dark oak, or some of each).

The attic rooms in the roof

Drain them on paper towels, and when they are dry you will find that some have picked up more dye than others, so that they look very natural when glued in place.

For a particularly neat finish, glue a strip of "corner angle" moulding along the ridge of the roof, and don't forget chimneys, cut from blocks of wood. Chimney pots can be short lengths of dowel, or you can buy real pot ones from the same suppliers who make tiles and bricks. I have to say that the chimney on my cupboard house bears very little relation to the position of any of the fireplaces inside, but then I am not overly troubled by logic in the dolls-house world. Atmosphere and effect are more important to me than realism.

This chapter is about my dolls houses and how I tackled problems I met while building them. The next chapter has suggestions to help you design one for yourself.

9 · Designing Your Own House

Before you start making plans for a house of your own, you need to understand a few principles of dolls-house design.

Access

An initial design problem, especially for anyone wanting to make a model of their own house, is that dolls houses can really only be one room deep. As soon as you try to make a house two rooms deep, you have to have opening walls on two sides of the house for access (front and back, or the two sides), and then you can never see the whole interior at once. It is also possible to have the house in two sections, hinged so that the two halves swing apart, and the front and back walls are fixed, but if you try to play with this sort of house, your people have to leap across a chasm to get from one half to the other.

Most houses in the United States open from the back, which allows for an elaborately constructed front, with wrap-around porches, gables and turrets. These houses are fun to play with and arrange, because when you look inside, all the details of the front are visible – the backs of the windows, the front door, and any alcoves created by gables or bay windows. The disadvantage is that a back-opening house cannot be placed against a wall unless it has castors underneath so it can be pulled out for play, or is set on a turntable. I prefer front-opening houses, which after all are in the best traditions of the old "baby houses" and cupboard houses of the 18th and 19th centuries.

Scale

There is some confusion in this country over which scale to have in a dolls house. Many old houses, and all the mass-produced children's houses and furniture, like Lundby and Caroline's Home, are in 3/4 scale (also called 1/16th), that is, with three-quarters of an inch in the dolls house equalling one foot in the real world. Collectors and miniaturists prefer the slightly larger scale of one inch to the foot (1/12th), and this is mostly what you will find in dolls-house shops.

When deciding on the size for your own dolls house, I strongly recommend that the house itself should be in 1/12th scale, even if it is for a child. Start by furnishing it with 3/4 size things, if you like, but as the child's tastes mature, you can strip off the garish Fablon she chose for wallpaper at age six, and begin to accumulate some better furniture and furnishings. I have friends with a growing collection of desirable miniatures housed in a box, while their children play with a dolls house temporarily furnished by Caroline's Home.

Because my own dolls house was built in a cupboard, I had no choice over the size of the rooms, and did most of my decorating by eye. It has ended up a rather grotesque mixture of scales: doorways only 4½″ high, a tiny piano from my childhood being dusted by a proportionately enormous, 5½″ tall maid, but because it has grown like that over the years, no-one seems to notice the discrepancies.

Perhaps this is the moment to discuss the difference between scale models, and dolls houses which are meant to be rearranged and played with. A model house scaled down exactly from a real one would have a ceiling height of 8″ or 9″ (20 to 23 cms), and would be about 16″ (40 cm) deep. In dolls-house terms this is simply not practical: it's too deep, and not tall enough. You can't get your hand right to the back of a room this size without knocking things over. For this reason, dolls houses are rarely more than 12″ to 14″ deep (35 cm), and have ceilings ideally about 10″ high (25 cm) or more, going down to 9″ or so (23 cm) on the top floors. No problem here if you are building a house that naturally has high ceilinged rooms, – Victorian, for instance – but a small Georgian manor will lose its proportions and shoot up into a tall, narrow town house. You can disguise a certain amount of the height with clever external details: lines of bricks or mouldings breaking up the facade, a raised doorway with steps below, or raised ground-floor windows with a false foundation making up the difference. Extending the house sideways will also help to balance the height, as long as you have room for a wide dolls house.

One last word on scale. I have recently lost my heart to ½″ (or

1/24th) scale. This doesn't sound very small, but if you visualise a square, with each side ½" long instead of 1", you will see that a house in this scale is one-quarter the size of a normal dolls house. Searching for furniture and furnishings in this size offers new challenge and excitement for anyone who has been a dolls-house enthusiast for a long time, and the very smallness of it all is irresistible. My first half-scale house can be seen in the

My half-scale house

photograph, in its usual setting, to give you some idea of the size. Beside it is an even smaller house, in 1/144th scale, and this too opens for furnishing. If you are interested in half-scale houses, you can get a very simple cottage from a firm called "Jack and Jill" for £12 (see under "Shops and Shop Fitters" at the back). Also available are a shop, a public house, and various double-fronted buildings, as well as an adorable backyard with privy, which costs

£6.75. Apparently one collector has set up a whole street of these houses with their backyards – an intriguing idea, and one that is perfectly practicable in this tiny scale.

Size

There is one Law of Dolls Houses which every owner will recognize, and that is that they are never big enough. Anyone who starts with a four-room, two-hallways design will be in despair in no time at all. Children are even more relentless about space, demanding bathrooms and nurseries, as well as a bed for every visible member of the dolls-house family, including any domestic staff. One solution is to open out the roof space, as I have already described, but better still, buy or build a three-storey house to begin with. My own dolls house has three storeys, two attic rooms, and still I have had to add to an extension, incorporating a kitchen, bedroom and roof garden.

Design

When planning a house, don't confine yourself to the central-hall-room-each-side design. Decide what rooms you want and arrange the house to fit. There is no reason why the front door cannot be offset, so that you have two adjoining rooms all the way up one side, with a single room on the other side of the stairs. This would mean that you could have, say, kitchen and skullery on the left of the bottom level, and a dining room on the right; drawing room and small study on the left of the second floor, main bedroom on the right, and so on.

Another idea would be to fix the upright partitions first, and then have different levels on the two sides, with flights of stairs connecting them. Many old houses ramble about in this way, especially when two have been converted into one.

What I don't recommend is trying to have two rooms running from front to back, divided by an archway, for instance. It is virtually impossible to reach the room behind without taking most of the furniture out of the front one. Sometimes I make a false wall at the back of the room which allows for a corridor outside, as I did in the dining room of my cupboard house. A small piece of furniture can be permanently positioned there, and an extra dimension is added to the room without the need for access.

Exteriors

I suggest being flexible in your approach to the outside of your house as well. The Georgian town house has been rather overdone as a design, although there are obvious good reasons for its popularity. What about an old castle instead? (Baronial hall, turret rooms, panelled bedrooms with secret passages). Or a pair of farm cottages, two up and two down, with brick fireplaces and contrasting styles of decoration in each.

If you are short on ideas, visit your library and look at books on architecture and country houses (or town houses), or take a camera and photograph a variety of house styles until one of them inspires you to the point where you can picture its interior, and get a feeling for its atmosphere. With this picture in mind, take up a pencil and start to draw. No need for artistic talent – you are just drawing boxes, as I did for Eleanor's house, described on p. 86.

A flat façade is the easiest for a beginner to design and build. Gabled projections are more difficult, though they can be made like an open box and simply glued to the front (this is how we made the front of Sally's shop, shown on p. 80). When faced with a problem like the awkward angles of a gable roof, I often make a mock-up with a piece of light card, folding and bending it to fit, then transferring the shape to a piece of plywood.

Even on a flat façade, you can have great variety and detail by using brick papers, paint and mouldings. Brick paper, which is available in Victorian red and also a softer Georgian pink, is applied with wallpaper paste. You can personalise it by picking out some of the bricks with water colour paints. It is a good idea to varnish the paper with a matt varnish, to prevent it getting grubby or rubbed. The edges can be protected with "coining", which is the line of stones down the corners of many Georgian houses. I made imitation stones for my cupboard house out of thick card, bevelling the edges with a craft knife. These stones can also be used to cover the bottom storey of a house, leaving the rest to be painted, as seen in many London houses of late Georgian vintage.

PAINT

Stones can also be painted on, the mortar indicated with fine lines, and individual stones picked out in varying colours. Even a simple painted exterior will look very effective if you choose your colours carefully, but I recommend silk finish or eggshell paint for sheer practicality. My friends who made dolls house kits, both initially painted their houses with matt emulsion, and after only a couple of hours of handling they were already finger-marked. An alternative solution is to apply a coat of varnish over the paint, and this is what they decided to do. If you are looking for a stucco effect, add a little fine sand to the paint, or apply it with a roller, which gives a gently dappled surface.

CLAPBOARD SIDING

Wood siding of the sort seen in the south-east of this country – and much used in the United States – is available in sheets four inches wide from suppliers who carry American mouldings. I found it easiest to cut the siding for my half-scale house by laying it flat and scoring it several times with a craft knife. When gluing siding, use an impact glue, and work up from the bottom of the house, avoiding joins as much as possible. Short lengths can be used up between windows (but keep the lines level right across the house). You might also consider using the siding only on the top or bottom half of the house, and painting the rest.

ARCHITECTURAL DETAILS

Although paint and paper are important factors in decorating the exterior of your dolls house, even more crucial are the architectural details. Even a strip of moulding, or a line of bricks, across an otherwise plain façade, can make a surprising difference. Many different mouldings are available from miniature suppliers, and some may be found in your local hardware store. The trim along the top of Sally's dolls house kit, shown on page 80, as well as all the trim on the outside of my own dolls house, was made from standard wood mouldings. Alternatively, make your trim from card, building up several layers where a thicker profile is needed. With card it is easy to cut curved shapes, like an elaborate fanlight for a door.

Wood or card strips can be stained (or painted and stained, see pp. 123–5), and applied in strips for a Tudor or Thirties house. Fill in between with imitation stucco, or brick paper, or perhaps make more realistic bricks by applying a thin coat of Polyfilla, scoring it with a sharp tool along a ruler, and painting the bricks individually.

Strips of moulding can also be used to make a portico around your front door. For pillars, either use dowelling, or the plastic pillars sold for wedding cakes. These are only 2" (6 cm) tall, but the ends are removable, so you can use several joined together to get the necessary length for your portico. On my house, I just made grooves in the front of two blocks of balsa wood to simulate the ridges of a pilaster.

WINDOWS

Don't neglect the external details of your windows. My dolls house has a very simple façade, and the windows are the main feature. I glued pieces of card above them painted grey to look like the decorative brickwork often seen on Georgian houses. There are window sills, made from a piece of moulding used upside down, and window boxes made very simply from strips of wood (card would do) and glued on. A proper Georgian house would have had windows of varying sizes on each floor: smallest on the top, and tallest on the ground floor, but I didn't know this when I made the house.

BALCONIES

These add a lovely touch to the front of a house. Real wrought-iron balconies (and area railings too) can be ordered to fit your own windows from John Watkins. They also make those shallow window guards that people used to have on nursery windows. If you can't rise to custom-made balconies, then I recommend the plastic ones sold by Hobby's. They are very cheap and easy to cut and, when painted, are indistinguishable from the real thing, though obviously a lot more fragile. If the front of your dolls house happens to open in one piece, rather than having two doors, then a balcony right across the first storey, with French windows opening out on this level, would give a lovely Regency touch. Or you could transfer the balcony to ground level, and make a porch.

STAINED GLASS

Here is another excellent personalising touch. There is a Dover paperback, *Dollhouse Stained Glass Windows*, which has lots of designs on paper that you colour yourself, but even better are the real stained glass panels sold by Wentways Miniatures. They are available in several styles and sizes, and again you colour them yourself, with spirit-based felt-pens. Use the panels in doors or windows, or buy one of their doors already made up with the panels: perfect for a turn-of-the-century building.

Foundations

I find that dolls houses are most satisfactory for play when they are raised up somewhat on a plinth. This can be made very simply from strips of wood glued under the house. You can set these flush with the existing walls of the house, paint or paper them to match, and create a false basement area with railings. Alternatively, have a shallower plinth, set in a little, and treat it as foundations. In my own dolls house I painted the plinth in a vaguely stoney colour, but you could make it more realistic with real stones cut from card or, for a more rural dwelling, glue on tiny pebbles (or lentils). Fill in round them with Polyfilla for mortar.

All the small touches I have mentioned make the difference between a mass-produced house and one you have designed yourself. Don't forget that you can add any of them to a house that you have bought, to make it more personal.

If you are prepared to tackle the woodworking side of making a dolls house, but can't face drawing up the plans, then you might consider buying plans. There are quite a few on the market: several in the Hobby's catalogue, including a very engaging "Crooked House" (for the Crooked Man), and a variety of mansions in different styles. Wansbeck Hobbies sell the plans for a solid Norfolk farmhouse, and Hobbies (Dereham) Ltd – not to be confused with Hobby's in London – have two excellent plans priced at under £2, one an Edwardian and one a Victorian house, both in 1/12th scale. Once you have any of these plans to give you confidence, then you can alter them to suit your own ideas. Check that they fit my general guidelines on height and depth of rooms, and adjust them if they don't.

It is wonderful to buy a ready-made dolls house and be able to start right in on the decoration and furnishing, but there is also

10 · Interior Decoration

Once you have your basic shell assembled, whether it is a house or a simple box, the next stage is to paint and decorate it, and it is much easier to do this before you fix in the windows or the stairs.

My first step is always to give the whole thing a coat of paint, inside and out. You can use plain white emulsion (called latex in the US) for this, and it will dry in a couple of hours. Next take some fine sandpaper (grit 150) and rub this painted surface all over to make it ready for wallpapering or the next coat of paint. You may wonder why it is necessary to paint before papering, but I have found that there is often some resin or oil left in the surface of the plywood which can bleed through the paper or fabric and leave a stain.

Ceilings

Ceilings are the next thing to be dealt with. I never use pure white paint in a dolls house, because I find it too cold and modern. Instead I either use one of the new off-whites that are on the market (like Dulux's Lily White), or more often make up a colour myself with what I have on hand – white silk vinyl with a blob or two of cream paint or brown stainer, for instance. This mixed paint I keep in a jar so it is always handy. All the ceilings get a second coat before I start on the walls.

Walls

You will probably want to paint one or two rooms in a dolls house, and for this you can use any leftovers of household paint. Small quantities can be tinted with Universal Stainers or even with tubes of artists' paints – water colours for emulsion paint, oils for oil-based varieties. I never use gloss paint anywhere in a dolls house. I much prefer the soft shine of a silk finish, or of semi-gloss paint like the small tins of enamel sold for model airplanes.

Most dolls-house shops carry special miniature wallpapers, but I rarely use them. I find that fabrics have subtler designs, and they

The sitting room in my cupboard house

are not as hard and reflective as paper. Even a heavily contrasted design, such as the Laura Ashley fabric used on the walls of my dolls-house sitting room, shown in the photograph, looks gentle and atmospheric. There is another, practical reason for using fabric on the walls, which is that 1/4 yard, or 25 cms will give you enough for the whole of a 9" high room. Dolls-house wallpaper comes in sheets 11" by 17" (28 cm by 43 cm) which are printed *across* the long side, so you may well need a sheet for each wall.

Spring and Summer are the times to go hunting for cotton material in the shops, or you can try using silk, Viyella, or any other fabric that is fairly firm. Stockists of quilting materials have excellent small-scale prints, and I have included two names of mail-order suppliers at the back of the book. You can send for a packet of mouth-watering samples in many colours and designs, some suitable for cutting up for borders or stair carpets.

For real economy, keep your eyes open in Oxfam and other charity shops for shirts, skirts, or dresses which can be used instead of new material. In one of these shops I once found a child's rayon dress printed with tiny figures and toys which made the most wonderful curtains, seen in the photograph of my nursery.

Sometimes I use wrapping paper on my walls, when I find a

The nursery in my cupboard house

striking design. One example is shown in the hall on p. 90 where I cut the wallpaper up and reapplied the borders as cornice and dado. Recently I found a sheet of wrapping paper which was printed with chinoiserie-style decorative panels which could be transferred directly to dolls-house walls.

To apply all wallcoverings, including fabrics, I use ordinary wallpaper paste. Don't ever use glue – besides being messy to apply, it can also stain the surface, and you will not be able to remove the paper or fabric should you change your mind. As well as the wall paper paste, you will need:

- scissors
- sharp craft knife (I use an Olfa with snap-off blades)
- paint brush, about 1" wide.

Mix up a small bowl of wallpaper paste, and while it is setting, get your fabric ready.

Measure the back wall and cut a piece of fabric to that size. You don't need to allow any extra, because the pasted fabric will stretch a bit. Now trim ¼″ (5 mm) off the bottom edge. If you find that the pattern of the material is printed out of true, just get it as square as you can, keeping any vertical lines straight, because these are what show. Using the brush, paste the back of the material, and the wall too. At this stage you will find that the pasted material has turned into a slimy, limp rag, but just lift it up and slap it roughly into place, papering right over the window and door holes. Then push the fabric around with your fingers until it is straight along the ceiling line. There will be a slight overlap onto the side walls. If this is more than ⅛″ (3 mm), take the piece of fabric out and cut a sliver off one side. The bottom edge should be a bit short so that there is a gap between wallpaper and floor. This will be covered later by a skirting board.

Next cut out your side walls and apply them in the same way. This time get the ceiling line in place as before, and try to fit the back edge neatly into the corner without overlapping onto the back wall. Any excess material can be brought to the front edge and trimmed off when it is dry. All this is easier than it sounds, because the fabric stays wet and slides around for quite a while.

Before leaving it to dry, just check that any upright lines or stripes are straight. You can manoeuvre them into place with your fingers if they are wobbly. Lastly, dab or wipe the walls gently with a damp cloth to remove any excess paste from the surface.

Your first room won't look too great at this stage. The paste will have oozed through the grain of the fabric, and the whole thing will be dark and sodden. When it has dried, you will find that, miraculously, there is no sign of the paste, and the fabric has tightened up and returned to its former self.

Now take your sharp craft knife and trim off any edges that stick out over the front. Cut round your windows and doors from the outside, so you can see what you are doing. Don't try to do this trimming until the wallpaper is really dry, or it will shift around. Once dry, it is as tight as the paper seal on a jar of instant coffee.

Your first room is now papered. Later you can add the skirting board, and a ceiling cornice if you like. If you find you don't like the fabric you have chosen, then you can whip it off, wash the pieces, and use them for something else.

One thing to remember when choosing wallpapers is to think of the house as a whole. You will find that it looks better if the rooms blend together, because as soon as you open the house they are all visible at once. When it comes to the inside of the actual front of the house, I always cover this with one large piece of fabric, rather than a patchwork of small pieces matching each room: after all, you only see it when it is opened. Sometimes I pick out one of the fabrics that I have used in a room, I choose a different but blending one.

Chimney breasts and fireplaces

When I am constructing a dolls house or room setting, I also cut out the chimney breast. I use an ordinary piece of pine, about 5" by 1" (12 cm by 2 cm). This I cut to the same height as the room, then I take a small piece out of the bottom of it to make the hole for the fire. The size and shape of this hole depends on the type of fireplace I intend to have, and some suggestions are shown in the drawings. If you don't have tools to cut thick wood, salvage a large piece of styrofoam packing material and use that instead. It is easy

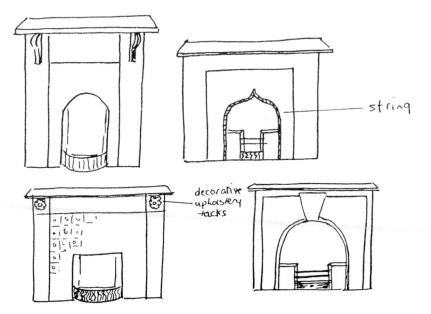

to cut, but benefits from being covered with paper to hide the texture. Heavy card can also be used, scored and folded to the right size and shape.

I wallpaper the wall where the chimney breast will go before putting it in (leave a gap in the paper where the back of the grate will be), then paste another piece of fabric and wrap it round the chimney breast block. This can then be glued into the room, but if you are intending to make your own fireplace, it is easier to do this while the block is out of the room. There are lots of simple surrounds that you can make quickly, and here are just a few:

(i) Buy some offcuts of balsa wood from a model shop, and make a basic frame. Smaller bits of balsa or card can then be stuck on top to make a relief effect, and a long strip glued to the top for the mantelshelf. For more detail, press a decorative upholstery tack into the two corner blocks. Once the mantelpiece has a preliminary coat of paint, it can be made to look like stone, painted wood, marble or any woodgrain, depending on your painting skills, although I confess that I can't manage any of the elaborate finishes myself. However, I did once have a great success with some leftover bits and pieces from a cold enamelling kit – I stirred two colours together and made some quite passable imitation marble (you can just see it in the photograph on p. 120).

(ii) Buy a length of picture frame moulding and make a surround, mitreing two of the corners (see fireplace on back cover). You can simulate any of the classic fireplace designs just by getting a different shape of moulding. To mitre the corners, I have a small mitre box and saw (see p. 56), but if you don't want to buy one, you can mark the 45 degree angle with a set square and cut it with an ordinary tenon (small-toothed saw. Any gaps can be filled in with Polyfilla before painting.

(iii) If the mitreing seems too difficult, buy a small wooden frame from woolworths and cut one end off. You may even be able to cut it in half and get two fireplaces out of it.

(iv) Build a fireplace out of real miniature bricks, available from the stockists I have listed at the back.

There are some tiny tile papers available from dolls house shops, and even real painted tiles. A little row of the real or the paper tiles around the fireplace, inside the surround, looks very realistic and appealing. You can also use a piece of paper or card, marbleised or painted to look like slate (use Zebrite grate polish, described below, to give this a soft grey sheen). In the house she made from a kit, Sally cut some glossy illustrations of wallpaper from a Laura Ashley catalogue and used these for tiles.

When the fireplace is completed and stuck to the chimney breast (I use a contact glue for this), spread some more glue on the back of the block and press it into place in the room. The little grate hole and the wall behind it can then be painted with blackboard paint, a dense matt paint that dries quickly, or you can paper it with brick paper. Finally, you can buy a length of decorative brass strip from the stockists listed at the back. Cut it (with a junior hacksaw) just a little bit wider than your grate hole, and wedge it in, bending it slightly. An alternative, which can be seen in the Christmas room on p. 30, is to cover a strip of card with some of the embossed gold paper sold for decorating cakes. Either of these will give you a slightly curved front to the grate, and you can pile up tiny scraps of coal or half-burned wood behind. For a different effect, cut two small blocks of balsa, and either push some nails into them as shown in one or two of the fireplaces that I have drawn, or cut a shaped piece of card to go in front. Whatever type of grate you make, a crumpled piece of red "silver" paper in with the coal will catch the light and give the illusion of a lit fire. This is so realistic that people often think I have put light bulbs in my fireplaces. You can, of course, install real bulbs when you are wiring the house: paint the bulb with the clear red acrylic paint sold in model shops, or use nail varnish.

A fender can be made out of more of the brass strip (choose a solid looking design), or with the gold cake paper glued onto card.

For those who can afford them, there are marvellous little stoves and fireplaces being made by craftsmen and sold through dolls house shops. If you buy one of these, or one of the cheaper mass-produced kitchen ranges, you can improve the appearance greatly by giving it a rub with some Zebrite. This is an old-fashioned polish sold in hardware stores for blackleading kitchen ranges, and when buffed it has a lovely silvery sheen. If you can't find it (it comes in yellow and black striped tubes), then pencil lead filings give a passable imitation. Pick out any details on the stoves with gold or silver fine markers.

Floors

Wooden floors can be made in several ways, but the simplest of all is to stain and varnish the plywood floor of the room. Do this *before* painting any internal walls. For the stain I use wood dye in walnut, oak or teak, then I varnish the floor, rubbing it down when dry with 000 steel wool dipped in wax. An even easier way is to rub on shoe polish in a suitable colour – try dark tan or mid-brown. I also use the shoe polish to modify a floor colour that has not turned out as I expected. Cover this floor with a sheet of paper held down with masking tape before you paint the walls or ceiling; in such a small space it is almost impossible to avoid touching the floor with your brush.

One of my favourite floor coverings is plain brown wrapping paper. I use the sort called Kraft paper, which has fine lines running through it, and stick it down with wallpaper paste. It can be scored with a pencil to imitate boards. You can also buy printed parquet or strip floorings, or one of the excellent tile papers sold in dolls-house shops. Any of these paper floorings are improved by a coat of varnish, or the plastic decoupage emulsion described on p. 143.

For a superbly realistic effect, buy thin strips of real wood, and glue them down with impact glue, using a pencil to mark nail heads and the ends of planks. You can see my first attempt at this type of floor in the attic bedrooms shown on p. 95. I used balsa wood which is rather woolly, and it didn't take the stain well, but it would have been improved by a coat or two of "sanding sealer" available from model shops. I once had excellent results making a floor with wood veneer. You buy this in sheets from model shops, and I cut it to size with a craft knife and glued it down with contact adhesive. (You can use it to panel a room too.) Any of the real wood floors can be varnished and wax polished.

Self-adhesive paper (Fablon, Contact) can sometimes make a cheerful flooring for a kitchen or nursery. The woodgrain ones are grossly out of scale, but I have often used the cork, and there are some tiny gingham ones that have possibilities. Another idea is to buy some white marbled paper and some black, cut them into small squares and stick them down alternately. This is more easily done outside the house on a separate piece of heavy paper – then cut the whole sheet to fit and glue it in. Sussex Crafts make a kit of pre-cut squares for one of these black and white tiled floors, and it is available from many dolls-house shops.

Model shops sell a roll of very thin real cork for railways, and this would be effective in a kitchen or bathroom, particularly in a modern house. Some of the colours in the Humbrol model range, sold in tiny tins, look very like linoleum, particularly numbers 78, MC 28 (green leather), and MC 29 (red leather), and the latter makes a pretty convincing quarry-tile colour as well. You can buy real quarry tiles or bricks, but they work out a bit expensive over a whole floor. In my own dolls-house kitchen I made a fairly successful fake quarry-tiled floor by first covering it with a slightly runny mixture of Polyfilla (spackle). When it dried, I painted it with tile-coloured paint, then scored it with a ruler and a nail. Finally I gave it a coat of varnish to bring up the surface.

Skirting boards (baseboards) and cornices

In my opinion, these are a necessity, not a luxury. Proper reproduction skirting boards can be bought from miniature shops or by mail order. These give a superb finish to a room, but even a cheap substitute, such as a strip of obechi wood or card, will make a crisp demarcation line between wall and floor and cover up any raggedy edges. Most skirting boards are about ⅝" deep (1.5 cm), but Victorian mouldings were generally deeper and thicker than Georgian ones, so you should bear in mind the proposed period of your house. I find the easiest way to handle the painting of skirting boards is to lay all the long strips down on some paper and paint them before cutting them to length (see p. 105 for my recommendations on paint). Move them somewhere to dry, or the paper will stick to them (I use a wire cake rack). When the paint has dried, rub them over lightly with some 000 steel wool, then they can be cut. A pair of dividers from a geometry set makes a good measuring tool. Open the dividers inside the room so the points touch the two corners of the wall, then remove them carefully and mark the skirting board with a prick to show you the length to cut. It's remarkably difficult to work with a ruler or tape inside a dolls house, and I find the dividers are much more accurate, particularly where short pieces are needed – around a chimney breast, for instance.

When the strips are cut to the right lengths, I glue them into the rooms with a contact adhesive. The real skirting board looks best if you mitre the corners, but it is a very fiddly job. I find the easiest way is to cut the lengths to fit right into the corners and then pare bits off with a craft knife till they fit together neatly.

While on this subject, I also want to point out that there are many other types of moulding that you can use in your rooms. A cornice makes a neat finish to the join between wall and ceiling, or you might prefer a picture rail, set an inch or so down from the ceiling. Even if you decide to add a picture rail after the room has been wallpapered, you will find that you can peel some of the fabric off by first cutting it with your craft knife along the lines where the rail will go.

Curtains and carpets

When you reach this point, you have finished with decorating and are on to the furnishing. In your own home, this is the moment when you move the furniture back in, hang the curtains and survey the room with satisfaction.

By now you probably have an idea of the type of furnishings you want, but you may be running out of energy. Those lucky people who are making room boxes are nearly finished, but the dolls house people can hardly see light at the end of the tunnel. I find that the thought of curtains looms over me so that I feel like giving up the whole project. What I tend to do is to put in most of the floors and carpets, and tackle the windows bit by bit. In fact I will be honest and admit that my own dolls house, which is more than ten years old, still has several uncurtained windows.

CARPETS

I think that velvet and very fine pinwale corduroy make the best carpets: real carpeting is far too thick. To make a wall-to-wall carpet, cut a piece of paper roughly the size of the room. Put it in the room and press it into the edges where the floor meets the walls, running your finger nail along to make a clear impression. Cut along these lines and use the paper as a template for cutting the carpet – but don't forget to turn the template over if you are marking the back of the carpet, or you will end up with a mirror image. I use wallpaper paste again to stick down all carpeting, including stair carpets; or you can use double sided tape.

Woven materials make good carpets and rugs: anything from tweed to printed cotton. Look carefully at paisley scarves and handkerchiefs, and you can sometimes see a miniature oriental carpet. Borders can be cut off and reapplied to make a better shape. Paste the bits to the floor or onto another piece of firm fabric, and pull some threads from the edges of the rug for a realistic fringe. Recently when I was browsing in an Oxfam shop I saw an Indian cotton dress, and the sleeves had bands of perfect oriental carpeting. Runners can be made from border designs for curtains, and Soleiado, the Knightsbridge shop that sells French provincial fabrics, has a wide selection in many patterns and colours.

Here are a few other ideas for capets using fabric: a child's handkerchief for a nursery carpet, dress fabric with a geometric or moorish tile pattern pasted over a whole floor, gingham – ¼" checks for mouse houses, larger for full size dolls houses.

NEEDLEWORK RUGS

Needlepoint or petit point makes fine oriental carpets. It can be worked on a variety of canvas sizes, depending on your eyesight and staying power, but somewhere between 18 mesh (i.e. 18 stitches to the inch) and 28 mesh is about average. There are several books on the market giving designs for needlepoint rugs and other projects, or a kit with charted instructions can be ordered from Jean Brown. This is designed to be worked on 18 mesh canvas, but a finer one could be substituted (giving a smaller rug, of course), and single strand crewel wool or embroidery thread used instead of tapestry wool. For the ultimate in dolls-house needlepoint, you can work with one strand of embroidery floss on 40 mesh silk gauze as in the two samplers shown in the photograph. I have tried it, and I can tell you that it demands pretty keen eyesight and some previous experience of needlepoint.

Beautiful and time-consuming rugs can be worked with tiny French knots on close-woven cloth. I have also seen hooked rugs made with a little device called a needle punch (available from Thames Valley Crafts). The loops can be sheared afterwards to give a plush effect.

I make very satisfactory imitation braided rugs with crochet, using four-ply sock wool which comes in soft tweedy colours, and a size 2.5mm needle. Start with a chain of three to ten stitches and then do simple double crochet (single crochet in the USA) round and round, increasing slightly on the curves to make the rug lie flat. According to the length of your original chain, you can make round or oval rugs in all sizes. Every few rows you change to a different colour to give the braided rug effect, and the whole thing goes very quickly – I can make several rugs in an evening. You can also plait strands of wool and wind them round to make a real braided rug, gluing the coils onto a base of aluminium foil, then peeling it off when dry.

Rugs cut from felt or velvet can be painted with dryish water colours or oils to look like Numdah or Chinese carpets, and fine embroidery gives a similar effect. For £2 or so you can buy a book with dozens of iron-on transfer patterns for rugs and other furnishings.

Needlework projects worked on different canvases

Woven oriental carpets which have the advantage of lying very flat, are available from Mini Marvels. Particularly nice are the stair carpets, in twelve-inch lengths. In my own dolls house I used striped braid on the stairs, of the kind sold at haberdashery counters for trimming clothes. It was about an inch wide, and I reversed one length to give a wider stripe up the middle.

CURTAINS

As I have already admitted, curtains are rather the last straw for me, so I have developed several systems for instant curtains, some in time-honoured tradition.

On many dolls houses you will notice that the curtains are nothing but strips of lace glued behind a piece of ribbon or upholstery gimp. To copy this, take a sample of your wallpaper along to a well-stocked haberdasher and choose lace of a suitable shade and width, usually between two and four inches. Look for a quality that resembles old hand-made lace, rather than a nylon one, unless you are making sheer net curtains. Antique markets are a good source of old lace and, bearing in mind that you need very little, rummage through the oddments baskets for old torn garments with lace still attached. Sometimes these pieces have only a narrow edging, but if the fabric is fine enough (silk, organza, muslin) you can use it to make the curtains, keeping the narrow lace as a frill down each inner edge.

Old net curtains can be cut up for dolls-house curtains, providing the mesh is very fine. The odd single curtain can often be picked up cheaply in junk shops. I can hardly walk past a second-hand or charity shop without flitting in quickly to see if there are any old silk scarves, handkerchiefs or shirts that can be adapted for dolls house purposes. All these old fabrics have the advantage of limpness. New ones stay bouncy even after repeated washings, and hemming the bottom makes the problem worse. For this reason I try to use a selvedge edge along the bottom, and I don't hem lace at all, but occasionally brush fraying edges with a weak solution of Evo-stick woodworking glue, which dries clear. You can also buy a product called Fray-Check from haberdashers.

If you are using material for curtains, rather than lace or net, look for fine natural fabrics. Polyester blends never hang well. To take the drip-dry finish out of pure cotton, wash it in a hot solution of 1/4 vinegar to 3/4 water. If you still can't get your curtains to hang the way you want, dip them in weak wallpaper paste and mould them into shape. They are immovable once dry, but for a permanent setting you can get excellent results. A similar technique is to pin the curtains onto a flat piece of styrofoam (or an acoustic ceiling tile), arranging the folds and drapes as you wish, then spray the whole thing with hairspray, or art fixative available from any art supply shop. Generally I prefer to sacrifice perfect drapes and folds in the interests of being able to open and shut the curtains.

PELMETS AND RAILS

Once you have your curtain material organized, you need to hang it up. Simplest of all is to glue it behind an improvised pelmet made of a strip of gimp or a piece of card covered with fabric. The card can be shaped to resemble an old-fashioned pelmet, with an extension either side which is folded behind the curtain tops to give a neat finish. (For all curtain gluing I use white glue, which leaves no stain when it dries.) This pelmet can be glued directly to the window, with the two extensions simply folded flat behind, but a better effect can be achieved by wrapping the whole thing around a long narrow block of wood, and gluing *this* to the window. Obviously curtains that are glued in place cannot be drawn open and shut – you either have them permanently open, or loop them back. To hold them back, I usually hammer in a couple of decorative upholstery tacks at the sides and wedge the curtains behind. You can see what I mean in the nursery on p. 107. Alternatively, you can tie them back with fine cord or plaited embroidery thread.

The obvious alternative to the pelmet variations is to use a curtain pole. You can buy a ready-made miniature pole complete with rings and finials, or you can make your own. Here are two methods:

(i) Buy some ⅛" (3 mm) dowel (model shops), two brass doorknobs (Hobby's), and two of the tiny screw eyes that picture framers use to take the picture wire. With your pin vice (p. 56), drill a hole either side of the window and screw in the two eyes. Cut the dowel about ⅜" (1 cm) longer than the space between the two eyes, so that it will stick out a bit either end. Now drill a hole in each end of the dowel, and glue in the brass doorknobs to make finials. To hang the curtains on this rod, I usually just turn the top over and make a channel to thread it through, sometimes leaving a bit at the top of the curtain to make a frill (look at the photo on p. 120). If you prefer, you can buy gold jump rings to serve as curtain rings, either

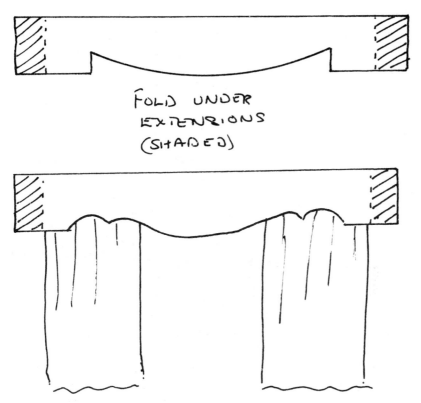

FOLD UNDER
EXTENSIONS
(SHADED)

from a jewellery supply shop, or from Wentways Miniatures, who also supply any other brass findings that you may need.

(ii) For an all-brass curtain rail, proceed as before, but instead of the dowel use ³⁄₃₂″ or ⅛″ (3 mm) brass tubing, cut it with a junior hacksaw, and glue the doorknobs into each end. The tubing is available from most good model shops at very little cost, or from Wentways Miniatures.

These curtain techniques can also be adapted for four-poster beds, and pieces of old silk and lace can be used to camouflage even a crudely improvised bed made of cardboard and dowels. Occasionally on my forays into antique shops I have been lucky enough to find small panels of hand-made lace which must have been used to decorate the front of a dress. These are often just the right size to make a canopy for a four poster bed, leaving enough to hang down an inch or so all round, as in the bed on p. 120. They can also be used to make a lace coverlet for a bed, with perhaps a brightly coloured bit of silk or a blanket showing through.

But now I am stealing information from the next chapters, which will give you ideas for furnishing your house, once it is built and decorated.

The main bedroom in the cupboard house

11 · Techniques for Making Furniture

How much furniture you actually make and how much you buy, depends on your personal ratio of time to money. Anyone who has a whole house to furnish is going to need a lot of furniture and artifacts, and you will find that money melts away in a dolls-house shop.

Here is what I recommend. Make a list of the sorts of things that have simple lines and can be made easily, and another list of things that are complicated or time-consuming. For example, a bed is easy to make, because it is only a box, and the bed-ends can be cut out flat. A chest of drawers, on the other hand, needs a fair degree of skill if the drawers are to fit neatly: so buy the chest of drawers, and make the bed.

Miniature shows and fairs are a great source of everything you need in a dolls house, and the dates of these fairs are published in both the dolls-house magazines listed at the back of the book. If you can get to one of the big fairs like Miniatura, held in Birmingham in March and September, you will see superb, high-quality furniture made by the very best craftsmen and costing sometimes hundreds of pounds, as well as simple basic pieces for a few pounds. There will also be stalls specialising in china, carpets, miniature baskets, dolls, fine lace and ribbons, and all the wood mouldings and brass fitments that you could ever need. I suggest that you go all round the show first, getting ideas and deciding where to put your money, then go round a second time and buy. If you buy immediately on impulse, you may turn a corner and find a better piece at a lower price. On the other hand, don't miss a real bargain. At the last show I went to, there was a basket of cast resin fireplace seconds, and they all went in the first hour.

My two friends who are making dolls house kits came with me to fair, and I was amused at how differently they approached the ness of stocking up. Felicity decided to furnish her kitchen , and she carefully chose a nice kitchen range, a Brambly

Hedge style dresser, a table and chair set (made in Taiwan, but good value for money), and a few small accessories. She also found a bathroom set, slightly damaged and vastly reduced. Sally bought pieces at random, avoiding ones she could make easily herself, and stocking up on small accessories, like baskets, that would add immediate interest. She also found an inexpensive counter and a cash register for the shop.

One other point about these fairs is that they often feature craftsmen at work. You can watch the experts turning tiny scraps of metal on a lathe, blowing glass, or cutting wood, and ask them for advice on your own projects. Miniaturists are like gardeners in their willingness to help, and I have never yet been snubbed, or told that a technique was a "trick of the trade".

If you have a lot more time than money, then make the little decorative accessories, like rugs and pictures, that give a dolls house charm and atmosphere. Improve the outside of the house with real slates and tiles made from card, and replace printed acetate windows with real glazing bars made from the inexpensive strips of square moulding from model shops. Try making some of your own furniture with the instructions that follow: you will be surprised at how easy it is, once you have taken the initial plunge.

All furniture designs in the next chapter can be made equally well from wood or card. Card is surprisingly strong when suitably finished, and is greatly preferable to a very soft wood like balsa, which will snap easily no matter how many coats of paint it has. I will give instructions for cutting and finishing both types of material.

Wood

It is tremendously satisfying to make your own furniture from wood. With a mitre box and saw, most straight cuts can be made accurately and simply, but for complicated, curved shapes you will need a fretsaw, an inexpensive tool which I have described on page. 54. Your model shop (or the stockists at the back of the book) will have obechi (a hard wood with little grain) and pine, in four-inch wide sheets of different thicknesses, as well as strips of different shapes for the smaller parts of furniture: square for legs, flat thin pieces for the sides of beds, etc. A two-foot long sheet of obechi, pine, lime, or American basswood which is similar to lime, will cost two or three pounds, and you will find you can cut quite a few pieces of furniture from it if you place them carefully. You can also buy walnut, American cherry, and mahogany, for very little more, but choose a sheet with a close grain that will look in scale in a miniature piece of furniture.

There are kits which have the wood already cut out, plus instructions for assembly and finishing. These are great fun to put together, and a good way of gaining confidence in constructing furniture. Most dolls-house shops stock kits imported from the United States or Germany, and Wentways Miniatures have some excellent ones of their own design, available in mahogany and other woods. There is also a range of Barbara Anne Miniatures, made in light wood to simple designs, and a huge Greenleaf kit which makes fifty-six pieces of furniture for £30. The wood in this American kit is rather rough, but the designs are good and, carefully finished, it certainly represents good value for money. For more of a challenge, order one of the furniture plans sold by Jennifers of Walsall.

FINISHING

The very first thing you must do before starting to assemble a kit or cut out your own designs from a sheet of wood, is to sand every inch of it until it is satin smooth. Use flour paper, a grey sandpaper of 240 grit, or buy one of the packs of English Abrasives finishing sheets for power sanders. Be careful to do all your sanding *with* the grain of the wood, not across it, and keep your paper flat when working on small pieces, or you may inadvertently round the edges. (For some shapes you may find it easier to lay the sandpaper flat on a table, and rub the wooden pieces on it.)

If you are using a light wood, and you want to stain it darker, then wipe it over with a wood dye before you glue it together, otherwise the glue forms a barrier and you will have white patches on your finished piece. These dyes are spirit-based so they won't warp thin pieces of wood; good colours are Blackfriars Teak for a light warm brown, and Dark Oak or Walnut for a deeper shade. Don't be tempted into buying the one labelled "mahogany" – it's a hideous purple red.

Once your furniture is stained and assembled, you need some sort of finish to create a polished look. I find that a very good result is obtained by painting on two coats of *button polish*. This is a pale brown form of French Polish (shellac), which can be applied with a small paint brush. Rub it down when dry with very fine wire wool (000 or 0000) dipped in furniture wax, to give a soft polished effect without the harshness of varnish. After the first coat of wax has been applied with wire wool, put on one or two more, until you have the degree of shine that pleases you.

If you don't like the button polish idea, buy a can of spray-on varnish, and give the piece of furniture a couple of light coats. This finish is also improved by the steel wool and wax treatment.

Furniture from card

Anyone who is afraid of using wood-working tools can make excellent furniture from card. This technique is particularly suitable for children, who are often very deft with their hands, and can get a lot of enjoyment out of constructing and painting furniture. To give you some idea of what can be done, in the photograph is a grouping of pieces of furntiture in 3/4 scale, all made from card by an artist friend of mine. Any of the patterns given in the next chapter can be traced or photocopied and used as templates. Glue the copy onto a thin piece of card first to give you a

Some furniture made from card

firm edge, then draw round it on heavy card. Picture mounting board, sold as "six sheets card", is a good weight, and offcuts can be bought cheaply from picture framers. Slightly lighter, but easier to cut, is Apsley board, or the kind that seems to come in fluorescent colours. The thinner the card, the more layers you will need. For example, the bed end on page 129 can be made of two pieces of Apsley board glued together, or four of the fluorescent card. Here is my system for all types of furniture.

Take the card, and draw on it as many outlines as you need to make the right thickness – say eight of fluorescent card for the two bed ends. Cut them all out carefully, then glue the layers together, four at a time, with white glue, and place them under a weight to dry. (I suggest putting waxed paper around them if they look likely to stick to their weights, or to each other.)

When the pieces are dry, give the cut edges a coat of polystyrene cement (model airplane glue). This dries very quickly and it soaks into the paper, making it stiffer so you can sand all the cut edges and bring them into line. (To sand inner curves, roll the sandpaper around a pencil or other round object.) The next step is to paint the pieces all over with a mixture of two parts emulsion to one of white glue. When this dries, you will be surprised at how firm the card now feels – quite like wood of the same thickness.

If you want a painted piece of furniture, then I recommend the acrylic paints that are sold in small jars in hobby shops. They have good colours, including some bright primary ones, and lovely subtle greens and blues. The brand name most commonly found is Tamiya, and you should find them with the small tins of Humbrol paint sold for model airplanes. (These are excellent for furniture too, but it is more trouble to clean the brushes, because you need white spirit).

Alternatively, if you have a nice selection of water colours or poster paints, then use these over a base coat of ordinary white household emulsion, or use the white as a background for some decorative painting: flowers, curlicues, or just fine lines. Finish off with a coat of varnish to protect the watercolour paint – either a matt polyurethane, or for just a few small things, buy a small bottle of artist's varnish in an art supply shop.

If you prefer the look of wood, then first paint the whole piece of furniture with yellow ochre paint. A tube of artist's acrylic is probably the simplest to use. Now take some varnish stain (walnut is a good all-purpose colour), and paint this over the dry yellow ochre paint. Leave the varnish for a few moments, then wipe or dab it with a paper towel or dry paint brush, until some of the yellow ochre starts to show through, giving the effect of woodgrain. If you get in a mess, then just drag the paintbrush across the surface, making the lines follow the lines of the

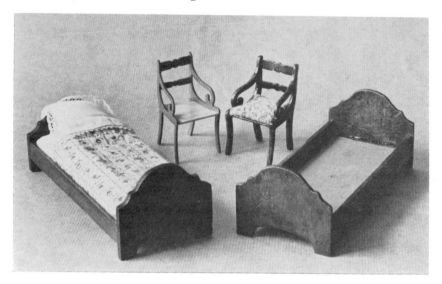

Wooden furniture on the left, card on the right

furniture. This finish is very effective and when well applied, can hardly be distinguished from a real wood finish. As you get more expert at it, you will find you can duplicate different types of wood grain by using a sponge or the tips of the paint brush bristles to manoeuvre the varnish. Any of these finishes can be softened by a rub over with steel wool and wax. In the photograph, the bed and chair on the right are made of card.

Dolls

Before starting on these instructions, I want to discuss one dolls house feature that is neither furniture nor accessory. No house or room is complete for me without its inhabitants. As I decorate the room, a sort of history of it develops in my mind, and it soon becomes clear to me what type of person or people should live in it. Some miniaturists maintain that the presence of dolls spoils the realism of a scene, and they prefer to leave evidence of someone having just left, or being about to arrive, but realism is not all that I am after. I want good detail, certainly, but also an indefinable dolls house atmosphere which makes me feel as if I am on the edge of another world, not just looking at a model.

Because I feel strongly about the presence of dolls, I am also very fussy about the ones that I am prepared to use. They have to have character in their faces so that I can believe in them. My favourite dolls are made by Jill Nix, and the shops that stock them are marked with a D in the list at the back. She makes all the heads, hands and feet by hand, out of Fimo, so they don't have the sameness of porcelain dolls made in moulds. The bodies, of cloth over wire, are fully poseable. These dolls are surprisingly inexpensive at £6 to £12, but you may be disappointed if you order them by post, because every face has a distinct personality, and you may not get a "person" that you like.

Slightly less expensive are the dolls made in Taiwan, and you can improve and individualise them by repainting the faces. New clothes will help too: use the ones they have on as a guide to size and shape. The world of china dolls ranges from these stiff Taiwan imports, through slightly more expensive kits, to the finest porcelain dolls with up to twelve joints.

12 · Instructions for Furniture and Accessories

These two sections are in alphabetical order for easy reference. I have only included furniture that is simple to make, whether from wood or card, hence no drawers. Items that are missing may be found in other relevant chapters, sacks under Mouse Houses, for instance. Check the index, if in doubt.

FURNITURE

Beds and bedding

I have given several patterns for bed ends. For a double bed, make the pattern wider by cutting along the line of dots, and inserting a piece of paper 1½" (4 cm) wide.

To make the body of the bed, I use several different methods, and I will start with the simplest.

(i) Use a shallow cardboard box of the right size – about 5" or 6" long (13–15 cm) and as wide as the bedhead, or slightly less. The depth of the box can vary between ½" to 1" (1–2.5 cm). Make a mattress out of a piece of foam cut to fit inside the box, and cover it with striped material to imitate ticking. Glue on the finished bed ends.

(ii) Scrounge a piece of styrofoam packing material from your local electrical shop, and cut it to the right size. Cover it with ticking material, and make a thin mattress from foam, gluing the *middle only* to the box. This keeps the mattress in place, but allows you to tuck the bedclothes in around it.

(iii) A length of balsa or obechi wood can be used in place of the styrofoam. Cover the wood in the same way, and glue the bed ends in place. For a more professional finish, you can stick sides on the bed made of wood, or card like the ends. If you are adding sides, then the bed itself needs to be made a little narrower so that the finished bed will not be wider than the ends.

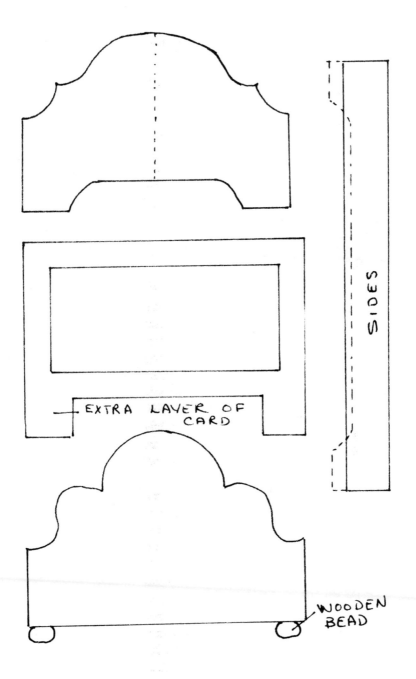

EXTRA LAYER OF CARD

SIDES

WOODEN BEAD

For covering mattresses, any striped material will do, and I use the remnants of a man's shirt that I picked up in a second-hand shop. It looks just like ticking, but is soft and worn. Sheets I make from men's handkerchiefs, using the hemstitched edge as the turned down edge of the sheet. I buy cheap cotton ones and put them through several washes until they have softened a bit, but best of all is an old linen handkerchief just on the point of disintegration. Pillowcases are made from another scrap of the handkerchief, again using the hemstitching as an edge, and sometimes with the addition of some very fine lace.

Blankets can be made out of any piece of flannel or fine wool that looks a suitable weight. Sometimes I bypass the blanket and just have a quilt. Dress fabric often has patterns that resemble patchwork, and I buy some whenever I can, and hoard it. Another idea is to buy gingham with small squares and paint a repeating design in the white squares with dryish water colours, or with any other paint that won't bleed into the fibres of the cloth. Cut the material wide enough to tuck into the two sides of the bed, but not at the bottom (too lumpy). 4½" square (11 cm) is probably about right for a single bed, allowing for seams. Make a bag out of two pieces this size, and stuff it with *very little* polyester batting or stuffing. Quilt it by sewing along the lines of the squares, through all the layers, making your stitches as small as possible.

Crocheted bedspreads can be made using 100 crochet cotton and a fine hook, and French knots look exactly like candlewick if worked fairly closely together. Old handkerchiefs or sections of old lace make effective and unusual bedspreads, so keep your eyes open in junk shops.

I recommend that all sheets be lightly anchored in place under the mattress with a few stitches. It stops them springing out, and dolls can easily be slipped in between the sheets.

Benches

I have given the pattern for the side of a bench on p. 131. To complete it, glue a length of wood 1¼" (3.5 cm) wide on top, allowing the ends to project slightly over the sides. As a further embellishment, run a narrow strip of wood under the seat, joining the two ends together.

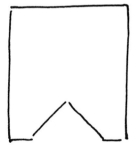

Chests

A blanket chest can be made using the same pattern as I have given for the bench above. You then need four rectangles of wood, two for the sides, and two for the top and bottom. Hinge the top either with little strips of leather, or with the real hinges available from the stockists at the back of the book, and from most dolls-house shops. In my hall there is a chest that I made years ago to this same design, but out of card, not wood. I painted it in shiny red lacquer, then glued on some oriental pictures from a book, and decorated the whole thing with gold paint. If I were making it now, I would first treat the pictures with decoupage emulsion (p. 143), to get rid of the excess paper on the back.

Chairs

(i) **Wooden.** I have given two chair shapes on p. 132, one simple, one ornate. The seat and the back splats are the same for both, but you can make the top splat more interesting with a shaped edge if you prefer. To upholster the seat, cut a piece of card fractionally smaller than the pattern, and cover one side with a small amount of padding (thin foam, cotton wool, polyester wadding). Wrap your upholstery material over the padding, and glue the edges under the card, then glue the card onto the seat.

(ii) **Upholstered chairs and sofas.** These are easy to make from one simple design, with variations. I have drawn two double patterns on pp. 134 and 135 which will give you four different designs of chair, ranging from a low, modern one, to a high-backed wing chair, and you can see all four in the photograph. (Trace or photocopy the designs, as before.) You also need a block of wood, or a piece of styrofoam, ¾" (2 cm) thick, cut to the seat pattern. To

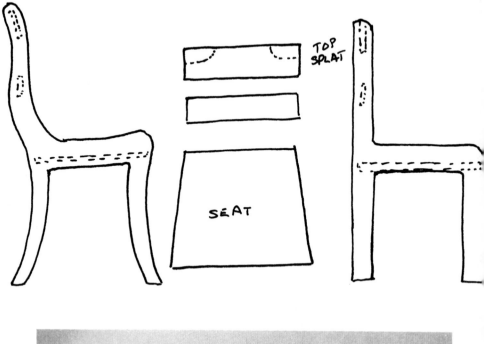

Two screens, and some simple upholstered chairs

make chairs 1 to 3 into sofas, extend the pattern in the centre back by two inches (5 cm) or more, and add the same amount to the width of the seat.

To make each chair, put two layers of your material (with right sides together) on a flat surface, lay your chosen pattern flat on it, and draw round the pattern in pencil. Now sew along these lines (preferably on a sewing machine, for strength), leaving the bottom edge open. Trim round your sewing, and turn the fabric cover right side out. Cut out a piece of card to the same pattern, pad one side by gluing on some thin foam or polyester wadding, and then slip the card into the fabric cover. At this point, stop and check that you have enough padding: thin cottons look better if you pad the back of the seat as well, and you may like to stuff a bit extra into the wings or the arm sections. Now slip stitch the bottom edge shut. On the original pattern, you will see that I have marked fold lines. Using a pencil, lightly transfer these markings onto the chair back you have just made, then sew along them, through all thicknesses. The back and sides are now complete, but still flat.

The seat is made by covering the piece of wood or styrofoam with a little padding, then gluing on the fabric covering. Only the top of the seat and one edge will show, so keep these neat and wrap any spare material under the block. Now spread some white glue on the sides and back of the seat, and wrap your chair back around it, holding it in place with an elastic band while it dries. A few stitches on the front edge of the chair will secure it.

This is the simple chair form, but there are some elaborations that I will also describe.

(i) Small wooden beads or spherical brass buttons make good bun feet for any of these chairs. They can be glued on, or held with tiny nails.

(ii) Add a frill all round the bottom. Make two or three rows of gathers along one edge of a strip of material 12" by 1" or so (30 by 2.5 cm), and glue it on.

(iii) Leave the chair seat unpadded and make a separate cushion instead. Use the top of the chair seat as a pattern but make it a little larger, then stuff it, and glue it to the chair seat with a little dab of white glue in the middle.

(iv) Cover all the seam edges with a trim made from a single strand of crewel wool, or a fine plait of embroidery thread. To make

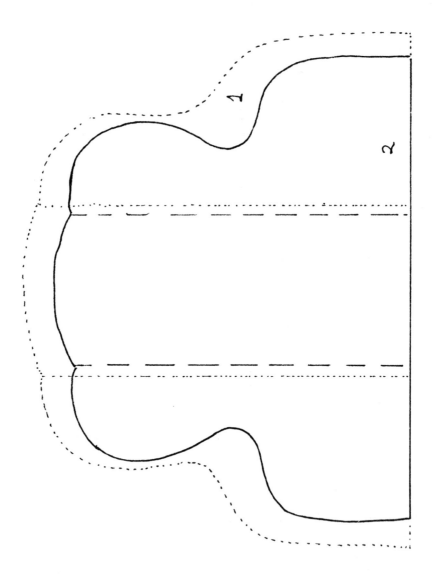

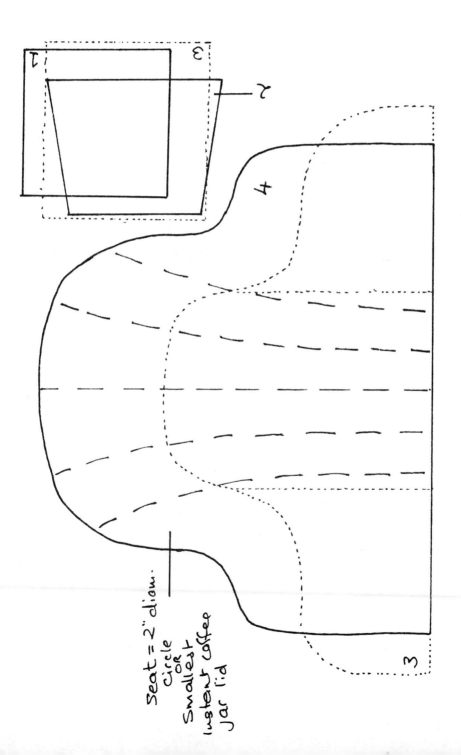

1

3

2

4

3

Seat = 2" diam.
circle
OR
smallest
instant coffee
jar lid

cording, take a long length of embroidery thread (I use two strands of different colours), fasten one end securely, and twist the other end until the coils are so tight that the cord can be doubled back on itself.

(v) Design no. 4 can be made into a button back. Glue the padding onto the piece of card that is your chair back, then place one of your two cut-out pieces on it. You now sew through fabric and padding with tiny dot stitches that show on the front of the material. When you have all the "buttoning" you want, place the other piece of fabric on top and sew round two sides. Turn the whole thing right side out, and slip stitch the last two edges shut.

Dressers

I have given a pattern for a simple type of dresser, avoiding drawers. The dotted line is a more interesting shape for anyone using card, or cutting wood with a fretsaw. If you want a shaped apron or cornice, use one of the designs for window pelmets given on p. 119.

Shelves

If you have alcoves on either side of the fireplace, then you can cut lengths of wood or heavy card to fit, and simply glue them in (use your geometry dividers to measure the gap and mark the wood or card). There will come a time, however, when you want a freestanding shelf – to make a kitchen mantelpiece, for instance (as in Sally's mouse wreath on p. 40). Cut a piece of wood for the shelf, and to make the little supports underneath, buy a length of full-size picture frame moulding. You will need very little, and may be able to scrounge an offcut from a local picture framer. Look at the end of the moulding to see its shape, and choose one that looks like a decorative bracket. Then, with your mitre box and saw, cut ⅛" slices off this moulding, paint or stain them to match the shelf, and glue the whole thing to the wall with an impact glue. Some mouldings have an extra lip which makes a rebate to hold the glass in place, but you can pare this off with a craft knife.

Sinks

The sink in my dolls-house kitchen was made out of a china bird feeder from a pet shop. The draining board is made out of a piece

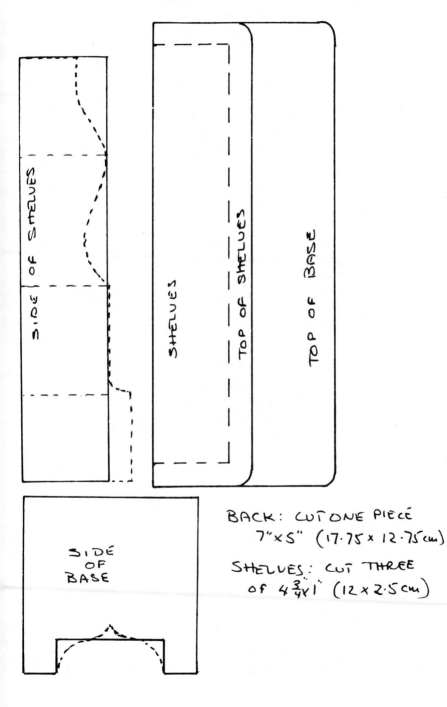

SIDE OF SHELVES

SIDE OF SHELVES

SHELVES

TOP OF SHELVES

TOP OF BASE

SIDE
OF
BASE

BACK: CUT ONE PIECE
7"×5" (17.75 × 12.75 cm)

SHELVES: CUT THREE
OF 4¾×1" (12 × 2.5 cm)

cut from one of those old-fashioned ridged paddles used to make butter pats. If you want to make a sink, I suggest using Fimo, although a passable approximation can be made by hollowing out a block of balsa, painting it with several coats of emulsion, and finishing with the "Porcelainit" paint sold for refurbishing baths.

The kitchen in my cupboard house

Drill little holes into the wall above to take metal taps. To be honest, this is one area where the commercially-made items are infinitely better than the homemade, and at the back is a list of some china workers who specialize in kitchen and bathroom fitments.

Stoves

Here again there is an enormous range of kitchen stoves on the market, ranging from very expensive handmade ones, to Taiwan imports. In between are the Phoenix kits which are fun to put together, but not suitable for a lot of handling by children. At the back of the kitchen in my dolls house, you can see the simple kitchen range that I made some years ago. The two ovens are simply blocks of wood with doors stuck on, the handles made from the brass clips used on envelopes. Between the two blocks I made a basket grate by hammering flat some pieces of soft wire from a garden supply shop. For cooking rings I used metal washers 1" (2.5 cm) in diameter, and I painted the wooden parts of the stove with blackboard paint, touched up here and there with gold marker pen to highlight the features. Any stove can be given an antique cast by an application of Zebrite grate polish, or pencil lead dust, as I have already described on p. 111.

Tables

These are invaluable in every room in the dolls house, and many can be improvised from oddments. For instance, I once made a table out of a piece from a broken chess set, with a mother of pearl counter as the top. Here are some more ideas:

(i) **Round, covered tables**. These tables are a Victorian feature that has lately returned to popularity. Any columnar shape will do for a base – a large spool, a small jar, the plastic container for photographer's film – it all depends on the height you want. For the top you need a jar lid of appropriate diameter. Now, measure for the material: run a tape up from the floor, across the top, and down the other side. Transfer this measurement to your fabric with a pair of compasses, or draw round a plate of the same diameter. Paint the back of the fabric with wallpaper paste, then mould it into graceful and permanent folds around your table. If your fabric proves recalcitrant, immerse it completely in the wallpaper paste, and this will subdue even the heaviest material.

(ii) **Plain tables**. A kitchen table can simply be a block of wood with legs glued to each corner. A more secure structure is made by adding an apron all round the table, as shown in the drawing on p. 140. This can be straight or shaped. A simulated drawer can be made by gluing a thin strip of wood onto the apron and adding handles – brass ones if you like, or white glass-headed pins for a simple pottery knob. All the shapes and sizes of wood needed to make a table can be bought in strips from model shops, so that you only have to cut them to the right lengths.

Fancy side-tables can be made in the same way, using a dark

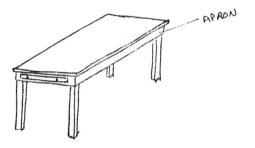

wood if you prefer, and perhaps some of the turned legs available from dolls-house shops.

(iii) **Trestle table**. For Sally's mouse house we made a very simple trestle table consisting of a flat rectangle supported by two pairs of crossed sticks, or struts. These struts were made from strips of wood 3/16" by 3/16" (5 mm) and glued where they crossed.

The ends of the struts had to be pared away slightly as I have shown, because they met the floor and the table top at an angle.

Washstand

I have given a simple washstand pattern which is simply glued together. Cut a round hole in the top for a basin, if you like.

Before leaving this section, I would like to mention that a lot of cheap imported furniture can be greatly improved by some simple refinishing. Take off the handles, and replace them with better quality escutcheon plates or knobs. Rub the piece of furniture over with 000 steel wool dipped in suitably coloured shoe polish (before replacing the handles), or in dire cases paint the whole piece with varnish stain, and then steel wool and wax it. The final solution is to paint the piece of furniture with a soft antique-coloured paint (Tamiya make excellent acrylic ones for model-painting see p. 125).

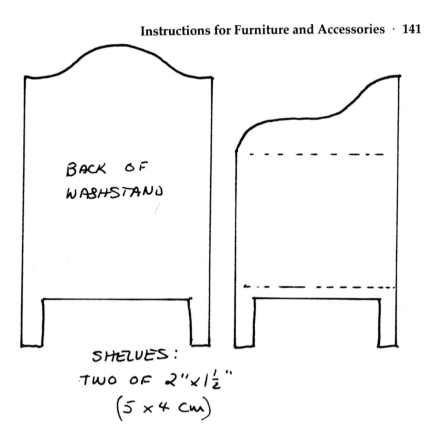

BACK OF
WASHSTAND

SHELVES:
TWO OF 2"×1½"
(5 × 4 cm)

ACCESSORIES
Books

One of my favourite rooms was the New York apartment shown on page 21, and in it was a wall lined with books. To mass-produce them, I used wood strips and the gummed coloured paper sold in packets for children. For the basic shape, I bought different thicknesses of obechi wood from a model shop – 1" by ³⁄₁₆" (2.5 cm by 6 mm) to make big, fat books, ¾" by ⅛" (2 cm by 3 mm) for the smaller ones. One long edge of all these strips was gently rounded with sandpaper to make the spines, then I wrapped the wood in pieces of the gummed paper, changing to a new colour when one ran out. All the strips were then cut into short lengths varying from ¾" to 1¼" (2 cm to 3 cm), to make books of different sizes. The saw marks on the top and bottom of the books gave quite a realistic impression of pages.

On the spines of these books I glued titles cut from illustrations of books in magazines, taken from my growing collection of advertisements for book clubs, illustrations of shelving systems, etc. Even the pictures that are out of scale can yield some lovely gold tooling – especially the ones for the more classy publications, like the Folio Society.

A simpler, but far less effective method of creating shelves of books is to find an illustration of a row of books and glue it to a block of wood. Individual books can also be made by gluing titles onto the tiny books with real pages which are available very cheaply from dolls-house shops.

New on the market are sets of books in kit form. You can choose from three different sets, and all come with the covers, bits of card to represent pages, and good instructions. They are available from Hobby's and many shops; although rather expensive at about £7, they are extremely realistic, and come in large sets of about fifty volumes.

Boxes

You can make cylindrical boxes (hat boxes, canisters) by the following method. Use lightweight card, about the weight of a manilla envelope or file card, and a piece of dowel or a round tin of suitable size (the ones that films come in are about right) as a form. Cut a strip of card long enough to go round the form with a slight overlap, and as tall as you want for your box (about 1″ or 1¼″ (3 cm) for a hatbox, for instance). Wrap this round the form and glue the overlap shut. Slide this cylinder down the form, and draw round it for the bottom of the box. Cut the bottom out and glue it on (you can neaten the join by covering it with string or thread, if you like).

To make the lid, cut a narrow strip of card (say ¼″) and wrap it round the form, *over* the first cylinder you made, which is still on the form. (This is so that the lid will fit on neatly later.) Glue the overlap, as before, and again make the top of the lid by slipping it down and drawing round it. Paint the lid and the box when they are dry and removed from the form. If you want the boxes covered in wallpaper, then I suggest you paste it onto the sheet of card before you start cutting out the box.

Carpets: see p. 114

China

This is a dolls house essential, for display of food, for decorating shelves and walls, and for simply standing around on tables. The beautiful sets available from miniature shops are expensive, and while you may be able to treat yourself to an item now and then, it is useful to have some ideas for cheaper, do-it-yourself china.

Anyone who has tried to make a tea-service from Fimo, or any other modelling compound, will understand why high prices are charged in the shops. Even with tips from craftsmen, I found my attempts very crude and unsatisfactory. If you want to try your hand at it, then press your plates and other items around forms to make them uniform. A plate from a plastic teaset can be used as a plate form. Dust the bottom lightly with talcum powder to stop the clay sticking, then press the modelling compound onto the bottom of the plate, and trim round it with a knife. When you remove the compound, you should have a passable image of the plastic plate. A china restorer recently introduced me to "superfine white Milliput" a two-part epoxy putty, available from Hobby's. It is easy to model and looks just like porcelain when dry.

A quicker and more satisfactory way of accumulating a lot of china is to buy a plastic or cast metal set. Take a magazine and wrap some masking tape or sellotape round it, sticky side up. Place all your items on this sticky surface, take it outside and spray it with white car primer paint, from a motorists' shop. Give it a couple of light coats rather than one heavy one that will sag and drip. The paint dries in minutes, and you can then spray the undersides. Now you have a matt white surface which will take any paint beautifully. For a glossy porcelain finish, varnish your decorated surface with modelling varnish. Plastic kettles and pans are greatly improved by being painted with the appropriate metal paint. Small tins are available from model shops, or use metallic markers.

An alternative to painting china is the découpage technique I have recently learnt. All you need is a bottle of Decal-it transfer emulsion from Hobby's, and some suitable printed designs. Look through magazines, wrapping paper, advertising leaflets and any other paper source for appealing designs that would look good decorating miniature pieces. The instructions are on the bottle, but briefly you paint your chosen design with several coats of the emulsion, and when it is dry, soak it in water for a few minutes to soften the paper backing. This can then be carefully scraped or rubbed off, until, miraculously, you are left with a transparent film printed with your colour picture! The film is flexible and slightly stretchy, so you can apply it to curved surfaces, using some more of the emulsion instead of glue. (You may find that very glossy surfaces need a rub-over with 000 steel wool before you apply the emulsion).

Cushions

Make cushions with miniature needlepoint, scraps of ribbon or printed fabric, or very fine lace. To trim the seams, use one of the techniques described for chairs on p. 133.

Display Boxes

Under this heading I include any of those shallow, framed boxes which were used to display collections of butterflies, shells, eggs, or even fish. You can make a fairly convincing box out of a matchbox tray, cutting the edges down to about ⅜" (5 mm), and painting the whole thing inside and out with blackboard paint. Make the very top edge gold, if you like. Inside you have a piece of white paper, with the items to be displayed set out on it. Butterflies can be painted on paper, then cut out. Bend the wings up slightly for a more realistic look.

   A collection of birds' eggs would be fun to make out of Fimo, moulding them from different colours, and painting tiny spots for the speckled eggs. A match box tray left untrimmed would be about the right depth for a fish made from Fimo. Make a glass for the box from the same clear acrylic used for windows.

Dolls House

No dolls-house nursery is complete without its own dolls house. You can just see one that I made from a matchbox on the left in the photograph on p. 107. The roof is a shaped piece of balsa wood, and the whole thing was very simply made with a craft knife. An N-scale house from a model railway shop would also make a good dolls house, or you could design your own from card, and just use the sheets of windows sold for N-scale buildings. Inside the house, glue in pieces of card to make the floors, and paint it all so it looks realistic, even if you don't go so far as to make furniture.

Dolls

By this I do not mean the inhabitants of the dolls house, which I have covered on p. 126, but the dolls they would play with in the nursery. Gifted workers of Fimo could attempt one like the cabbage patch doll in my dolls-house nursery, or a simple baby doll, with a Fimo head and the limbs all concealed in a gown. Eric Horne makes some beautiful, tiny jointed peg dolls, which are stocked by The Mulberry Bush, amongst others.

Food

Fimo modelling compound, which comes in lots of different colours, including a transparent one which alters the other colours, can be made into any sort of food. Fimo has to be warmed to make it malleable, and I cheat by placing mine for a few seconds on the side of my stove to warm – much quicker than working it in your hands.

Good tools to use in doing the modelling are toothpicks, pins, manicure tools, and a wire brush (dab the Fimo with it for an orange peel effect). Sweets can be made by putting strands of suitable colours together (red and white for candy canes, black and white for humbugs), rolling them out till they reach the right size, then chopping bits off.

Fimo is baked to make it hard and permanent, and afterwards it can be sanded or filed if necessary. There is no noticeable shrinkage in the baking, but unsupported pieces may droop, because the Fimo softens slightly before it hardens.

Apart from Fimo, there are other similar products on the market – Cernit is one – or you can use a compound such as Das, or Milliput, and then paint the finished object. A coat of modelling varnish improves the final appearance of anything that would naturally have a glossy surface.

Bread is most effectively made from bread dough, which can also be used like Fimo for general modelling. My first recipe had a lot of salt in it, which made the mixture absorb moisture from the atmosphere. One day I opened my dolls house during a damp spell, and found that my large and lovingly-made collection of food and china had exploded. I have also heard reports of bread dough objects being eaten by mice, despite layers of paint and varnish.

For the undeterred, here is the recipe:

- 3 slices of white bread (the more "plastic" the better)
- 3 tablespoons white glue
- ½ teaspoon glycerine

Remove the crusts, shred the bread, and mix it with the glue and glycerine. Grease your hands with glycerine and knead the mixture till smooth. You can mix any paint into the dough to colour it, or paint it when dry. The mixture dries out quickly, so keep any that you aren't using in a plastic bag.

Metal accessories

Hobby's catalogue has a list of nearly fifty metal accessories, ranging from a bust of Wellington to candlesticks and frames. They cost only pennies, and have a lot of detail that shows up very well when painted.

Before painting, you must go over all the pieces with a metal file, or some sandpaper, to remove the burrs and rough edges left by the casting process. Eleanor and I found this satisfying and fun, and she was very handy with the file. The next step was to stick them onto a piece of tape rolled round a magazine with the sticky side up, then we took them outside and sprayed them lightly with car primer. This gave a good matt white surface for the final painting, which was done with the paints sold for model airplanes, plus the occasional touch of fine gold marker pen. I love these markers: the gold gives a finish much more like real gold leaf than any of the paints one can buy, and I often use the pens to go over frames and other accessories that I buy ready "gilded".

Lately there has been a glut of metal accessories like bicycles and birdcages, all painted bright pink or blue, and available from almost any gift shop. Don't spurn them. Repainted in more appropriate colours they look remarkably good, and many are just the right size for a 1/12 scale house.

Pictures

An excellent source of all styles and sizes of pictures is an art catalogue like the Athena one, available from any of their shops. In it you will find maps, sporting prints, Old Masters and modern paintings. You can also use sections cut from Christmas cards, or you may prefer to use the illustrations of the cards in the charity brochures that flood in through the post before Christmas. Advertising material and magazines often have suitable and unusual pictures, but make sure that the illustration is square, not taken at an angle, and without shadows.

There are many alternative ways of framing pictures, ranging from found objects like tiny brass curtain rings and metal washers, to wooden ones cut from lengths of moulding with your mitre box and saw. A great variety of mouldings is available from the stockists I have listed at the back. When making a wooden frame, I recommend that you cut the picture you plan to frame slightly larger than you need. Then you can glue the pieces of the frame onto this backing, which is easier and more secure than just glueing the mitred corners together.

Pretty metal frames are stocked by most dolls-house shops, or they can be ordered from Hobby's catalogue. They come in all shapes and sizes, and are also suitable for mirrors and photos. Gild them with gold felt markers.

Several years ago, when I was faced with having to create some grand family portraits for a dolls-house dining room, I devised an inexpensive and simple framing system. The portraits themselves came out of a small book on Gainsborough that I bought very cheaply in a book sale. To frame them, I took a piece of heavy card, and cut a rectangle the size of the outside of the frame. Then I cut a window in this rectangle which was the same size as my picture. The frame was about half an inch wide all round, and before sticking the picture behind the hole, I covered the whole frame in some of the embossed gold paper strip sold for decorating cakes. I folded the paper over the edges as well, to hide the card. When the painting was glued behind, I had an impressive family portrait in what looked like a gilded plaster frame. If you can only find this paper in silver, you can colour it easily with a gold marker. (One of these frames can be seen in the open room on p. 30.)

For mounts for water colours or prints, buy a small pad of ingres paper from an art supply shop. This will give you pages of subtly textured, coloured paper. For glass, use the thin acrylic sheet used for glazing windows, or purists can buy real glass (for photographic slides) only 0.5 mm thick (less than 1/32th of an inch), from

Wentways Miniatures.

Needlework catalogues have pictures of samplers and tapestries that look very effective when framed. You can also create a sampler by painting it with very fine felt tips on close woven cotton. When you write on the fabric, the grain creates tiny irregularities that look remarkably like embroidered stitches. For a photograph of a real sampler, worked on ✕40 silk gauze, see p. 116.

Plants

There are innumerable ways of making plants, from Fimo, from bread dough – even from quilling paper. I will describe one or two of the techniques I have used myself.

First there are the real plants that look in scale in a miniature setting. In the photograph, you will see by the hand a tiny sedum (a rock plant) and an air fern, both live plants. The pots themselves are stocked by many of the dolls-house suppliers. Next come the ones made from dried plants or flowers: look around a good florist for a supply of these. Finally, I make some myself. The easiest

Plants: two live, the rest home made

technique I found, was to buy some artificial fabric leaves with wired stems. and trim them to resemble potted plants. You can see the palm I made by just snipping into the leaves with sharp scissors then bending them into graceful shapes. The other plant was made with green florists' tape. I used two thicknesses of tape, with some fine wire sandwiched between – these plants are more limited in shape because of the narrowness of the tape.

Screens

In the photograph on p. 132, you can see two screens, both made on the same principle. The oriental one was made out of a Ling greetings card which was already marked with panel divisions. We glued it onto some heavy, mounting board card, using an impact glue to avoid warping. The sections were then cut apart with a craft knife and a metal ruler, and glued onto fabric to make a backing and provide hinges. We used a piece of dark red Viyella, but any floppy material will do. Set the sections of the screen about ⅛" (2 mm) apart when gluing them to the fabric, so that there will be plenty of leeway for folding. Colour the bare edges of the card with black or gold felt markers.

The scrap screen was made from some wrapping paper that we were lucky enough to find already printed with scraps. Failing that, you could use oddments of wrapping paper or illustrations from magazines. We gave the surface a coat of decoupage emulsion to make it glossy, and decorated the edges with scallopings of gold marker pen. Alternatively, you could cut the edges off strips of gold cake decorating paper.

Toys

Many toys are listed in the Christmas chapter, most of them made from Christmas tree ornaments. Others that you might like to make are: a skipping rope with handles made from Fimo, or from wooden beads with a bit of toothpick stuck into one end; pull-along animals made up from a small wooden animal (sets of them come in matchboxes) with black press studs (snap fasteners) glued on for wheels; a farm set from the HO gauge section of your model railway shop; building blocks cut off a length of ¼" (6 mm) square moulding, and painted with letters (the wood surface gives a slightly blurred finish that is very realistic). Dolls and dolls houses I have listed separately.

In a way, it seems a pity to end this book on such a practical note, when the point of dolls houses and miniatures is that there is something for everyone, even the least practical. It was years before I began making my own furniture, and even now I keep to simple shapes and techniques, occasionally treating myself to one of the beautiful, craftsman-made items that can be found in shops and shows. For me, it is the creating of an ambience, a particular atmosphere, that is the fascination of working in miniature. As a room or house begins to come together, and I can see who lives in it and what goes on there, excitement grows in me until I become single-minded to the point of obsession. All my concentration is focused on one small point of interest, while around me confusion grows. Meals are late, tools and materials spread themselves all over the kitchen, so much so that my son Daniel approached the table with his plate the other day and asked "Would you mind if I ate my lunch on your workbench?"

Much of this interest stems from my childhood, when I believed in fairies, and every gnarled root looked as if it had a tiny door in it. The miniature world seemed to loom around me, as if I had swallowed one of Alice's potions, and this sensation comes back when I am in one of my dolls-house phases. I was sitting in a coffee shop recently, staring at the table cloth while talking to a friend, when I realized that I was looking at perfect miniature rush matting. Only white paper, of course, but stuck down with wallpaper paste, and coated with a mixture of yellow ochre and white paint. . . .

You will probably find, after a few weeks of thinking in dolls house scale, that all sorts of "found" objects will jump out at you and shout "flower vase" or "table top". You may discover a new interest in hardware stores, as you browse amongst the rivets and washers. Soon it becomes difficult to throw things away. Magazines might have pictures, or book covers, or designs to transfer to plates with "decoupage". I couldn't even get rid of an old valve radio the other day without opening the back to make sure that there was nothing useful inside.

Not every miniaturist gets involved to such an extent: your interest may begin and end with a Christmas mantelpiece scene, or a few pieces of furniture grouped together, but there is a tendency to expand. The few pieces of furniture grow into a collection that needs a room or house to display it. You find a friend with the same interest who will share ideas and trips to shows and dolls-house shops, or possibly discover, as I did, that one of your children becomes that friend, so you can enjoy a great common interest and excitement together. This is the marvellous thing about Miniatures as a hobby: it appeals to all ages, and to people with very different skills, or even none at all. Within the framework of a dolls-house or miniature room setting, there is something for decorators, designers and artists, for needlewomen and carpenters, for total beginners as well as experts – in fact, something for everyone.

STOCKISTS

DOLLS HOUSE SHOPS

I have included all the shops I can find, even the ones that have smallish stocks. They are listed by area. Before making a long journey I suggest you telephone the shop as quite a few have limited opening times. Many of the shops have mail order catalogues; send a stamped addressed envelope for details.

Guide to symbols: T: telephone first (for opening hours, or appointment to visit a showroom). K: particularly good range of dolls house kits. D: Jill Nix dolls stocked.

LONDON

Dolls House Toys Ltd, 29 The Market, Covent Garden, WC2E 8RE, 01-379 7243
Kristin Baybars, 3 Mansfield Rd, NW3, 01-267 0934
Newson Gallery, Windmill Hill, Enfield, Middlesex, 01-363 3675
The Singing Tree, 69 New Kings Rd, SW6, 01-736 4527
Tiger Tiger, 219 Kings Rd, SW3, 01-352 8080

SOUTH-EAST

G&B Butler, 48 The Pantiles, Tunbridge Wells, Kent, 0892 22684
Donettes, Antique Market, 52 Bridge Rd, E.Molesey, Surrey, 01-979 3552
Dorking Dolls House Gallery, 23 West St, Dorking, Surrey, 0306 885785
The Mulberry Bush, 25 Trafalgar St, Brighton, Sussex, 0273 493781 (K)
Nick's and Bob's Miniatures, Willowherb, 52 Station Rd, Stoke
    D'Abernon, Cobham, Surrey, KT11 3BN, 0932 66966
Reflections, 88a High St, Tenterden, Kent, 05806 4678

EAST

Clair's Crafts, 4 Rosemary Rd, Clacton-on-Sea, Essex, 0255 424317
Marion Clifford, St. John's Cottage, Church St, Ryhall, Stamford, Lincs, 0780 63175 (T)
Minimus, 52a Newham Rd, Cambridge, CB3 9EY, 0223 352026 (T, K)
Wansbeck Hobbies, White Lion St, Holt, Norfolk, NR25 6BA, 0263 713933 (K)

SOUTH-WEST

The China Doll, 31 Walcot St, Bath, Avon, 0225 65849

Miniature World, 37 Princess Victoria St, Clifton, Bristol, B88 4BX, 0272 732499 (D)

Tiny T'ings, 884 Christchurch Rd, Boscombe, Bournemouth, Dorset, 0202 429891

Tridias, 6 Bennett St, Bath, Avon, BA1 5BG, 0225 64970

WEST

Dolls and Miniatures, 54 South St, The Barbican, Plymouth, Devon, 0752 663676 (D)

The Doll House, 5 The Esplanade, Fowey, Cornwall, PL23 1HY, 072683 2606

Torbay House Miniatures, 11 The Quay, Exeter, Devon

MIDLANDS

Cranhill Designs, Knowle, Nr Solihull, Birmingham

El Encanto (Mexican accessories), 29 Loseby Lane, Leicester, 0533 57719

Jennifers of Walsall, 108 Caldmore Rd, Walsall, 0922 23382 (K)

Lillian Middleton, Days Stables, Sheep St, Stow-on-the-Wold, Glos, GL54 1AA, 0451 30381

Minnie Maria Miniatures, 2 Mansell St, Stratford-upon-Avon, Warwickshire, 0789 67612

Moorland Miniatures, 7 Stockwell St, Leek, Staffordshire, ST13 6DH, 0538 383814 (T)

Parkinsons of Broadway, 32a High St, Broadway, Worcs, 0386 853527

Rumplestiltskin, 12 High St, Watlington, Oxfordshire, 049161 3294

NORTH

Carol Black Miniatures, "Sun Hill", Gt. Strickland, Penrith, Cumbria, CA10 3DF, 09312 330 (D, T)

Fiddly Bits, 24 Kings St, Knutsford, Cheshire, WA16 6DW, 0565 51119

Fossgate Crafts, 37 Fossgate, York, YO1 2TF, 0904 38265

"Lovin'Givin' ", Marple Bridge, Cheshire, 061 427 7460

A Small World, 36 Turnpike, Newchurch, Rossendale, Lancs, BB4 9DU. 0706 213637

SCOTLAND

Royal Mile Miniatures, 154 Canongate, Royal Mile, Edinburgh, EH8 8BN, 031 5572293

MAIL ORDER (Many shops have mail order catalogues. Send SAE)
Hobby's, W. Hobby Ltd, Knights Hill Square, London SE27 0HH 01-761 4244

Hobbies (Dereham) Ltd, 20 Elvin Rd, Dereham, Norfolk, NR19 2DX

Thames Valley Crafts, 51 West St, Marlow-on-Thames, Bucks. SL7 2LS, 06284 73892

SUPPLIERS

Books:

(all these titles are stocked by The Mulberry Bush, 25 Trafalgar St, Brighton, Sussex – separate catalogue.)

Furnishing Dolls Houses, Audrey Johnson, London: G. Bell & Sons, 1972

Landscapes in Miniature, John Constable, Guildford: Lutterworth Press, 1984

Needlework in Miniature, Virginia Merrill & Jean Jessop, New York: Crown Publishers, 1978

Baskets

C&D Crafts, 133 Lower Hillmorton Rd, Rugby, Warwickshire, CU21 3TN

Brass furniture fittings

John J. Hodgson, 25 Sands Lane, Bridlington, North Humberside YO15 2JG

Miniature Crafts, "Tumbleweed," Drove Lane, Cold Ash, Nr Newbury, Berks. RG16 9NL

The Mulberry Bush, 25 Trafalgar St. Brighton. Sussex 0273 493781

Wood 'n' Wool Miniatures, Yew Tree House, Silverdale, Carnforth, Lancs. LA5 0RB

Building Components

Borcraft Miniatures, 8 Fairfax View, Scotland Lane, Horsforth, Leeds, LS18 5SZ (hundreds of wood mouldings)

Terry Curran, 27 Chapel St, Mosborough, Sheffield, S19 5BT (tiles, bricks and other clay components)

Dolls House Emporium, Park Hall, Denby, Derbyshire DE5 8NB (moulded plastic windows and doors)

Hobby's, Knights Hill Sq, London SE27 0HH.

Ann Shepley, 20 Tilford Rd, Farnham, Surrey GU9 8DL. (Victorian tiles)

Sussex Crafts, 6 Robinson Rd, Crawley, W. Sussex, RH11 7AD (general and plumbing components)

Carpets

Mini Marvels, Caprishaw Ltd, 25 Crescent View, Alwoodley, Leeds
LS17 7QF (woven orientals)

China and Pottery

Avon Miniatures, Wayside Cottage, 262 Turleigh, Bradford-on-Avon,
Wilts. BA15 2HF (porcelain kitchen and tableware)
Muriel Hopwood, 41 Eastbourne Ave, Hodge Hill, Birmingham B34 6AR
(plain and decorated ceramics)
Lenham Pottery, 215 Wroxham Rd, Norwich, Norfolk NR7 8AQ
(bathroom and kitchen fittings and china)
Ann Shepley (bathroom sets and tiles), *see under* Building Components
Stokesay Ware, 37 Sandbrook Rd, Stoke Newington, London N16 0SH

Dolls House Dolls

Jill Nix dolls in shops marked ''D''
Marie Beglan, 41 The Furrows, Walton-on-Thames, Surrey
(similar to Jill Nix, from £26)
Jane Davies, Amber, The Street, Walberton, Nr Arundel, W. Sussex
BN18 0PH (porcelain, £10–£40, up to 12 joints)
Dolls House Corner, The Haven, 65 Oakbury Drive, Weymouth, Dorset
DT3 6JG (porcelain, £10–£15)
J Designs, Dolls House Dolls, 4 Ruvigny Gardens, London SW15 1JR
(porcelain, £40–£60)
Sunday Dolls: *see* Needlework. (Swallowhill kits from £8 and clothes
patterns)

Electrical Fittings

Hobby's, Knights Hill Sq, London SE27 0HH
The Mulberry Bush, 25 Trafalgar St, Brighton, Sussex
Thames Valley Crafts, 51 West St, Marlow-on-Thames, Bucks. SL7 2LS
Wentways Miniatures, West End, Marden, Kent TN12 9JA
(Tiffany shades)

Fabrics

(For wallpaper and curtains – all cotton. 7 first class stamps to each firm
below for huge range of tiny prints)
Strawberry Fayre, Chagford, Newton Abbot, Devon TQ13 8EN
Village Fabrics, 30 Goldsmiths Lane, Wallingford, Oxfordshire
OX10 0DN

Glass

Leo Pilley, Chy-an-chy, St. Ives, Cornwall

Kits (furniture)

(X-acto, Realife, Mini-Mundus, Chrysnbon sold by many dolls house
  shops. Particularly large selection at Jennifers of Walsall).
  Independent designers:
Barbara Anne Miniatures, Unit 3 Lowes Farm, Kelling, Holt, Norfolk,
  NR25 7EB (simple designs, pale wood)
Wentways Miniatures: *see* Electrical Fittings. (light or dark woods)

Kits (dolls house)

(Most shops stock some kits)
Dolls House Emporium, Park Hall. Denby, Derbyshire
Jennifers of Walsall, 108 Caldmore Rd. Walsall
Minimus, 52a Newham Rd. Cambridge CB3 9EY

Magazines (First two have dates for Miniature Shows)

The Home Miniaturist, Mrs Mary Churchill, Foxwarren, 18 Calvert Rd,
  Dorking, Surrey RH4 1LS. £9 for six issues.
  (Many instructions for beginners)
International Dolls House News, P.O. Box 39, Leamington Spa, Warwicks.
  CV32 5FY. £8 for four issues, U.S. $15 bills, or $15.75 cheque.
  (Of particular interest to collectors of old houses.)
Nutshell News, Boynton & Associates Inc, Clifton House, Clifton,
  VA 22024, USA. Overseas subscription (12 issues) airmail: $64, surface:
  $34. (Nearly 150 pages of information and instructions, colour photos).

Metal Components

Miniature Crafts; *see* Brass Fittings. (decorative brass strips, tubing, etc.)
Wentways Miniatures: *see* Electrical Fittings. (rods, tubes, wire)
John and Valerie Watkins, 21 Fair View, Chepstow, Gwent NP6 5BX
  (ironwork: balconies, railings)

Metalworkers

Country Treasures, Rose Cottage, Dapple Heath, Admaston, Staffs
  WS15 3PG (fine range of brass and copper accessories).

Needlework Supplies

Jean Brown, 54 Woodbrooke Rd, Bourneville, Birmingham B30 1UD
   (kits for needlework carpets)
Carol Black Miniatures: *see* shops (patchwork kits)
Royal School of Needlework, 25 Princes Gate, London, SW7 1QE
   (✳38 silk gauze, sold by square inch)
Sunday Dolls, 7 Park Drive, East Sheen, London SW14 8RB
   (silks, lace, fine ribbons)
Thames Valley Crafts, 44-46 West St, Marlow-on-Thames, Bucks.
   HP14 4LX (needle punch kit)

Quilling

Mrs Pat Green, Past Times, 115 Broadway, Duffield, Derbyshire,
   DE6 4BW

Shops and Shop Fittings

Sid Cooke, Unit 5, Winyates Craft Centre, Redditch. Worcs B98 0LA
Jack and Jill, "Drybones", Burgh Lane, Chorley, Lancs.
   (also half-scale houses)
Jennifers of Walsall, 108 Caldmore Rd, Walsall. (counters, shelves etc.)
Thames Valley Crafts: *see* Needlework Supplies above.

Silver

Gordon Blacklock, 18 Countisbury Rd, Norton, Stockton-on-Tees,
   Cleveland TS20 1PZ
Ken Palmer, 124 Willmott Rd, Sutton Coldfield, W. Midlands B75 5NW

Stained Glass

Wentways Miniatures: *see* Electrical Fittings

Tools

Hobby's, Knights Hill Sq. London SE27 0HH
Jennifers of Walsall, 108 Caldmore Rd, Walsall
The Mulberry Bush, 25 Trafalgar St, Brighton, Sussex
Tilgear, 20 Ladysmith Rd, Enfield, Middlesex EN1 3AA
   (hand and power tools, many special offers)

Wood (for furniture)

Borcraft: *see* Building Components

Jennifers of Walsall: *see above*
The Model Shop, 6 Westminster House, Kew Rd, Richmond, Surrey
The Mulberry Bush: *see above*
Wentways Miniatures: *see* Electrical Fittings

INDEX